# Navigator of the Soul

## Mitchell Kastros

Michelle:
thank you for all the
smiles and friendly greetings.
Best wishes always and
take good care.
Mitch Kastros
2-18-05

**VANTAGE PRESS**
New York

Please send comments to the author at joebeefs@earthlink.net.

*Cover design by Polly McQuillen*

Published by Vantage Press, Inc.
419 Park Ave. South, New York, NY 10016

Manufactured in the United States of America
ISBN: 0-533-14759-X

Library of Congress Catalog Card No.: 2004093564

0 9 8 7 6 5 4 3 2 1

On September 11, 2001, you brought us out of our funk. It is now up to us to stay out of it. My tribute to you is to try and live up to the challenges of everything I have written.

This book is dedicated to the 343, and to the family I have had the opportunity to grow with and be a part of through training, acquaintance, and friendship. When you drop by the station while visiting our town, I am in awe. During our visit you make me feel equal, but when you leave I know I do not deserve to wear anything that says "FDNY."

# Contents

# Preface

The historical events that took place on September 11, 2001, thrust our nation into a state of total perspective. The things that are truly important were at the forefront of everyone's thoughts and actions. On that day and the days that followed, for what hopefully will not be too brief a period, the residents of our great country stood as one. Our freedom, which perhaps had been taken for granted by many, and was now threatened, forced a lot of us to reacquaint ourselves with reality, and our own mortality and vulnerability. No longer were we immune to the horrors, which until now were always someone else's problems, somewhere else. The word "hero" has been used more than we can recall, yet directed by the masses to a different segment of our society. Our heroes were no longer being found on the playing field or the big screen, which seems to be the case most of the time. In essence, the entire country dialed "911" all at once, and each member of every fire department, police department, and emergency rescue agency in the United States was called upon to be there, no matter where he or she happened to be.

The praise we have received is looked upon by many of us as unjustified and undeserved, for people feel this way about those of us who are thousands of miles away from "Ground Zero" and the Pentagon, and we are only wishing we could have been there. These actions are in some way helping you get through this as part of the healing process, and that is good. You praise us for what we do and what we are prepared to do, but it is our job, and for some of us, our life. We're not being heroes. It's just what we do.

What you may not realize is that your calling upon us has resulted in new or renewed responsibilities, commitments, and ownership on our part to be just as worthy of your praise if you ever need us in the traditional sense or you happen to see us in action. What you may realize even less is that through your response toward us, you have helped us to heal as well. We have been hurt, as all of us have, losing hundreds of our fellow brothers and sisters in the tragic events that took place that day. In light of your response, you are just as worthy of our praise, and also deserving of our thanks, for you are doing as much for us as you say we have done for you. You are our heroes, for when you call us, you are facing potentially life-changing challenges that can be met only with the type of inner strength and character that many of us only wish we possessed. Your exhibition of this strength and character helps shape and mold our own lives and inspires us to respond in the same way should we ever be challenged as well. This is what a true hero does for people.

As we all know, the media attention with regard to September 11 has been directed for the most part to the firefighting, police, emergency rescue, and other public service communities. However, we in the services are well aware that many, many people in all walks of life have contributed, without fanfare, much to the healing and rebuilding of our nation's spirit and new "norm."

As time continues to pass since the attacks, it seems we need to remind ourselves of how we felt as we witnessed the events of that day and the days that followed as we tried to get back to "normal." What was important then is just as important now, and we cannot lose sight of or discount it. We can't afford to keep things in perspective only when we get kicked in the head, and we cannot forget those who were lost (the citizens, our public servants, and those in the military), the loved ones who were left behind, and those who continue to fight to protect our freedom.

Hopefully this small book will provide some simple insights to a better, healthier, happier and more enjoyable life, which is what all of us who truly deserve it are entitled to. We will often look at life as a journey, with happiness as the journey itself, not the destination, but with some directions.

This book is not the result of years of study or the methods and ideas of doctors, philosophers, psychologists, or other accredited authorities. The teachings in these chapters are from people who taught themselves to find health, happiness, peace of mind, and self-worth. They also did something about their problems by accepting the responsibilities for their actions and decisions. They realized at some point that fairy tales may have happy endings, but real life doesn't. It just ends, and the key is to be happy to the end and to do it on our own at no one's expense.

So strap on your seat belt, take off on the journey into yourself, and take this opportunity to say hello to roads you may have already traveled, or a path that has few tracks but may be the one you want to be on. The change of scenery may do you good.

Bon voyage!

# My Thoughts on 9-11-01
# Written in October 2001

On September 11, 2001, at about 6:45 A.M., I was on duty at the fire station, finishing the last couple of hours of what had been a fairly uneventful shift. The first of the crew to rise, I had already showered and dressed and was about to complete some unfinished business from the day before prior to our scheduled staff meeting at 8:30.

It was at this time that the phone rang, still too early for a routine business call, so I anticipated it being someone needing service, though probably not an emergency. The voice on the other end responding to my greeting was that of an adult female. She was polite, yet abrupt as she requested to speak to my partner who was still asleep, along with the rest of the crew. I didn't think too much of it as I woke him with the announcement of the person holding on the line (it was his mother) but then recalled that I did detect some concern in her voice. As I went about my business, I told myself to observe my partner later to see if there might be something bothering him that may have had something to do with the phone call. I didn't have to wait, because shortly after giving him the message, he called my name, directing me into the living room where he had turned on the television. Entering the room, I saw what had been the reason for the concern in that woman's voice on the phone. At the same time my partner told me that an airliner had just crashed into the World Trade Center in New

York City. I don't recall what my response was at that particular moment, if there was a verbal response at all. I just remember watching what was taking place live and then learning of the events that led to the smoke, flames, and destruction that we were observing.

By now, the rest of the crew was up and had joined us, watching in disbelief as another plane deliberately crashed into the second tower of the World Trade Center. The room echoed profane single word exclamations as each person who was now watching the screen expressed how they were feeling about what they saw. During these particular moments, I knew I was silent, but continued to watch as both towers were now engulfed in fire raging from tens of thousands of gallons of jet fuel.

I now had three concerns. First, that people were able to escape the buildings; second that emergency personnel were not putting themselves at tremendous risk, and finally, that the buildings remain intact. Fortunately thousands of people were able to evacuate the buildings and the area without being seriously injured. But as the first tower crumbled to the ground, we knew that thousands of citizens and many firefighters, police officers, and other rescue workers had just lost their lives.

My next thoughts, which would be for the most part my only thoughts for the next eleven days, were expressed as I said softly, "My brother is going to this." My youngest brother Andoni is a member of the Sacramento Urban Search and Rescue (USAR) team. I don't know if anyone responded to what I said because I immediately went to my bedroom to try and contact him on the phone. I was connected to his personal voice mail and left him a message, letting him know I was thinking of him, that I loved him, and that if he was going to this incident, to be careful. The fact that I didn't reach him was a strong indication that he was going, which was confirmed later that afternoon when he called me from his rental car as he drove from San Diego to Travis Air Force Base in Sacramento in six-and-one-half hours (you do the math). He was attending a USAR meeting in San Diego at the time of the attack and was unable to take a plane back to Sacramento because all commercial aircraft had been grounded.

After attempting to reach my brother, I returned to the living room at the firehouse, where a fairly large group of firefighters had gathered in front of the television. I think it was at this time that we all observed the second tower collapse. A few minutes later, I picked up the ringing phone as the fire chief called to let us know that she would probably be late for the staff meeting, as she was in a briefing with the police chief and city administrator concerning the events that had just taken place. We ended up conducting most of the meeting without her, somehow managing to get through it accompanied by the tragically historic dialogue coming over the television in the next room.

The rest of the day, though technically a day off, was going to be a busy one nonetheless, even without the events that had just taken place. Most "days off" are pretty busy with business commitments, household duties, and other activities that make up a good piece of life. At times, the busy schedule is very frustrating, drawing us away from the simple pleasures that help us enjoy and appreciate life as we should. Right now the simple things are all that seemed to matter, as should always be the case, with home as the place to be, together with family and true friends.

The next several days involved some adjustments at work as far as a heightened awareness of so many things. We, as firefighters, tried to prepare for possible terrorist attacks in so-called target areas of the Monterey peninsula, as well as other parts of the state. A incident similar to New York and Washington, D.C., anywhere in the state would most likely involve our department in some way. We also had to deal with a great deal of emotion on the job, something that could be dangerous in our attempts to perform effectively. Our family of brothers and sisters had been severely impacted by what took place back east, and huge efforts were being made by all of us to try and stay focused. We still had a job to do because the world did not stop with the attacks. It would not be fair to the people we serve to respond to their needs with any less enthusiasm and precision as they had been accustomed to, nor deserved. The emotions and sense of loss that we were experiencing had to be addressed out of the public's view. In fact, we had an added responsibility to help people restore faith and hope, and otherwise nurture their own emotions, as we were suddenly now a large part of people's attempts to heal.

Personally, I tried to respond appropriately to whatever needs people had as I tried not to dwell too much on the fact that my brother was working on "The Pile." I knew what hours his team was off duty, so we spoke briefly by phone during that time each day, mainly just to make sure he was all right. Though the calls were pretty bland, it was a great feeling to hear his voice every day, if only for a moment. The routine was broken though, as later during his stay, Andoni told me that one of his friends from FDNY died in the line of duty at the World Trade Center. He seemed all right talking about it, which I hope will be the case as time goes on. On Friday, September 21, Andoni returned with his team from New York City, much to the relief of a grateful family. Instead of labeling one of his travel bags with his own last name, Andoni put the last name of his fallen friend and brother, Mojica, on the bag as a tribute. Our sincere thanks to Chief Doug Rogers of Sac Metro

Fire for personally providing us with updates and status reports, and to Deb from Task Force 7 for all of the e-mails. Upon Andoni's return, we spent the weekend in Sacramento, enjoying food, family, and friends.

While he was away, my every thought was on Andoni and his well-being, but also on the safety of the entire team. Since he became a firefighter in Sacramento in the early 1990s, I have had the honor and privilege, through what is called a "ride along" program, to train and work with many members of the Florin, American River, and now Sacramento Metro Fire Department. This program allows firefighters to work shifts at other fire departments to learn procedures and training methods that can benefit their own departments. This opportunity has allowed me to learn a lot about firefighting, but has also given me a chance to get to know a lot of good people and make a couple of very good friends. I treasure these relationships very much and appreciate the time we spend together.

Ironically, I have been with my brother as a crew member in both of the two critical incident stress debriefings that he has been in with his department. The first was for a major traffic accident that gained state recognition on December 12, 1997, and the second was the following summer for a swimming pool accident that claimed the lives of two toddlers. Being together on these counseling sessions was important and helpful to both of us. In all likelihood, he will be involved in a third session in the not-too-distant future without me. However, I am there at a moment's notice if and when he needs me, one way of the two-way street that makes up our relationship.

The events that have taken place since September 11 have generated emotions and actions that seem to be all-too scarce under so-called normal conditions. People have united as one, exhibiting patriotism and compassion, grief, anger, and a spiritual awareness unlike anything any of us has ever witnessed in our lives. At the moment, the world is in sync with a total perspective on what is truly meaningful. Firefighters, police officers, and other emergency rescue and support people have been placed on pedestals, showered with public praise, and looked upon as everyday heroes, much the same as professional athletes and entertainers, who themselves seem to feel this way about us as well. People stop by the fire station to say hello and compliment us with adoring words about what we do and how much we are appreciated for it. They wave to us as we drive the streets in our fire engine, deliver baked goodies, and send us flattering greeting cards. Firefighters who have worked the disaster scene back east are being thrust into the media spotlight by being invited onto talk shows, and a television show about a station in the New York City Fire Department is being shown, partly to raise money for the firefighter relief and rebuilding funds. It's as if the entire country called 911 at the same time and we did a good job. Whether we are in the middle of the action in New York and Washington or mopping the floors in the engine bay here, everyone seems to feel as if we have personally been there for them.

Patriotism is in vogue and highly fashionable, as the American flag, in all sizes, is the hottest selling commodity in the country. Coffee cups, antenna balls, T-shirts, hats, and videos boasting the stars and stripes are already on the shelves of every type of retail outlet imaginable. The Grinch has stolen Christmas, but everyone in Whoville is holding hands and singing as if something has happened, because until that something happened, this was never the case. With each passing day since September 11, more and more pomp and circumstance have surfaced, clouding our vision to where we seem to have lost sight of what has taken place, what is currently taking place, and what is yet to take place. There is talk of getting back to "normalcy," whatever that happens to be. Is normalcy what we had before those magnificent towers came crashing to the ground? Was a complacent and overconfident nation populated by a largely selfish society normal? Furthermore, was a catastrophic event such as this the only thing that could possibly shake this society enough to finally grasp an awareness of what is really important? Sadly enough, are we willing to think we have started to heal in just a few short weeks and that this will never happen again, even if we don't retaliate? We are at war, wounded and bleeding, many literally, yet we insist that things go back to normal immediately.

Perhaps those who do not have a close connection to what happened are healing quickly and getting back to normal, but there are many thousands who are still hurting very deeply and will continue to do so for a very long time. They don't have the opportunity to deny what has happened because it is too fresh and too visible. While most of us are enjoying the luxury and illusion of quickly getting back to normal, thousands of funerals are being planned and taking place, many without the remains of those who died. Attempts at closure by many families of those lost that are being conducted without the bodies of their loved ones are leaving huge voids that will make the healing process so much longer than "normal."

The entire firefighting and law enforcement community, for the most part, is still grieving the loss of hundreds of their brothers and sisters who lost their lives in the attack on September 11, and will for quite some time. Normalcy for most of us is a long way away, due to the common bond that we all share, from the smallest volunteer fire station to the huge metropolitan department that runs tens of thousands of alarms each year. Fires burn as hot in the small village as in the big city, and the pain and suffering of the sick and injured know no geographic limitations. The bullet from the gun of a criminal pointed at a police officer will travel just as fast no matter where the trigger is pulled. The empathy that we feel for the families of our fallen siblings is real, spontaneous, and unrehearsed. Our own families, to a fair degree, live in fear that someday we may not come home as well, due to a bad day at work. Therefore they feel the same as the rest of us toward the families who are suffering through the sorry reality that is now theirs.

In our jobs as firefighters, complacency leads to disaster, and being insensitive is an injustice to the people we serve. The events of September 11 have forced us into a different focus and mindset, but many citizens who loved us a few weeks ago are now criticizing us for being too cautious in situations that cause them certain inconveniences, because they feel that something of this magnitude could never happen here.

Our nation was recently caught in a state of complacency that it will hopefully never be in again. We were fooled into thinking that we could never possibly experience on our soil what has taken place and that our freedom would never be threatened in such a way. How wrong we were to think this, and how foolish we will be to assume that only highly populated areas of strategic and political influence are the targets of the cowards who have set out to impose their way of existence upon us. The landmarks and buildings such as the World Trade Center and Pentagon are not the targets. The minds of every citizen in the country are the targets, and all of them have been hit, whether we choose to think so or not. Getting back to normalcy may include the opening of airports and financial markets, the resuming of professional sports, getting back to school, and a semblance of routine, comfort, and health each of us was accustomed to that made up our daily lives. However, getting back to old behavior habits and old ways of thinking should not be a part of getting back to normal. The values that seemed so important to all of us during the height of recent events need to be as important on a daily basis as time goes by and not be so easily forgotten by those who were not directly affected. The kindness, support, patriotism, and spirit that people have exhibited for each other and the country need to remain strong and not surface only as a reaction. While you are waving the flag, the easy part, wave your heart and soul as well. If you are not used to it, you will find it to be more of a challenge, but it's doable.

Part of a normal way of life should include developing the ability and having the willingness to face and accept new challenges that have been presented to us and to meet them head on. We are in a time of uncertainty that may last for quite a while. It is unfair and unwise to expect a quick fix in an attempt to recapture everything we had prior to the attacks in New York and Washington, D.C. Hanging onto the nationwide spirit that appears to be so strong at this time may be just as powerful a force against our enemies as any military weapon we may use against them. What has happened has caused many people to behave differently, which at this time is perhaps more normal than anything you may be wishing for.

In spite of all of the opinions and thoughts expressed here, I speak for many firefighters by saying that we truly do appreciate the public recognition that seems so unparalleled. Although the media focus at this time is on our industry, we know that these incidents have affected everyone, and we realize that you are helping us as well. Our shift is doing everything possible to make sure we do not create any disillusionment to even one citizen who looks up to us for any reason, needs a helping hand, or wants to express his or herself in such a way that it promotes healing on both sides of the street. We know there are a lot of fragile hearts out there right now, and we want you to feel as good about what you are doing for us as we do about what we are doing for you. We indeed hope that your healing process is a rapid one and that you will be able to help others heal. May you somehow gain strength from what has happened and find a way to bounce back.

# Some Keys to Feeling Better

1. Be easy to help.
2. Marry only for love.
3. Don't try to be Superman, 'cuz you ain't.
4. Choose your friends carefully.
5. Choose your battles carefully.
6. Choose your heroes carefully.
7. Leave the toilet seat down.
8. Do something every day to please someone.
9. Be nice.
10. Be happy.
11. Be patient.
12. Respect yourself and others as you would yourself.
13. Learn to take yes for an answer.
14. Say "please."
15. Say "thank you."
16. Have fun.
17. Let people know how you feel about them while you and they are still here.
18. Incorporate some sort of teamwork into your day.
19. "Stressed" spelled backwards is "Desserts."
20. Avoid unhappy people.
21. Keep a plunger handy.
22. Don't let your past, good or bad, dictate poor treatment of yourself and others.

# 1

# An Overview

Firefighters are provided with an opportunity, and for those of us who choose to take advantage of it, the luxury of being able to keep things in their proper perspective every day. Each alarm that we respond to is a reminder for us to count our blessings, not sweat the small stuff, and stay in touch with our mortality. Any of us, no matter who we are or what we do, could be gone at any time. Every time we roll to an incident, someone is experiencing a bad time, and our petty concerns and what we think are important problems are not so important at this time. Based upon the severity of the incident, they are usually not important at just about any time. We are in a position where we have to think of others first. For those of us fortunate enough to not have to force ourselves to do this, it is not just a duty being performed but also a big part of a life within a life being lived.

We see birth, death, and all aspects of life in between, only with none of the bullshit. In an emergency, all that matters to those we are serving is that the situation gets better, that it gets back to "normal," something that was so important in the days following September 11. The life within the life of a firefighter around the firehouse is no different from that of anyone else. He or she is part of a family that might own a family business, in most cases spending twenty-four hours at a time together, about ten or eleven times a month. We do chores, eat and sleep together, just as any family is supposed to do. As a business, we work together on projects and training, and interact with and serve our customers when they need us. We are, foremost, a team, whether referring to the family, the business, or perhaps in terms of a ball club that trains and practices to perform well on the field.

No matter what situation we find ourselves in, we need to function as a cohesive unit in order to be successful. Whether it's doing routine chores around the station or entering a burning building, we need to work together as a crew, a family, and/or a team, depending on the situation, but always with the attitude of "one for all." Small, seemingly insignificant actions that most people don't even recognize, are paramount in the team-building process, which subconsciously could mean the difference in someone's life, be it a person we are serving or one of our own. It's all a matter of getting to know each other, learning the best ways to treat people, and utilizing the best each of us has to offer that will get us through the shift. It helps us to not only meet, but also conquer and exceed the challenges that we face each day, and also plays a huge role in our own personal development. The good crews learn that a good attitude will get them through a lot, and that the great things that can be accomplished through good communication, unselfishness, patience, and the ability to listen are endless.

The appointed (family) leaders, the captains (big brothers and sisters), and chief officers (mothers and fathers) who empower their troops rather than attempt to control them are the ones who earn respect and trust. These true leaders become in a sense, heroic, because what they are transcending is helping to build and shape solid teams (as well as individuals) on a foundation that is so strong, it defies all attempts of compromise from any direction, be it from within or outside the unit. They set a positive tone and show their strength through fairness and compassion rather than through trying to instill fear because they are afraid themselves.

The lives of firefighters are indeed no different from the lives of anyone else. We come from different family backgrounds, face the same challenges, experience the same ups and downs, and respond according to how we are put together. We are taught lessons by our parents and guardians, and if we are fortunate and a little lucky, the lessons we learn help to guide us on a journey that however challenging it may be, is rewarding nonetheless. We are hopefully taught that we are the navigators of our souls through the teachings of our parents and other people of influence, but most importantly through the teachings of ourselves. If we are able to effectively guide ourselves through this journey called life, then we are truly fortunate.

In essence, firefighters have two lives, the one we live at home and the one we live on duty. Although the two places we live in are different, who we are deep inside remains the same, and the person we are at home is the same person we are on duty. Though our behavior may be appropriate and professional to our customers, which is what they need, our true personalities "at home" in the fire station will surface, especially over time. As we are human, we act human, and our behavior patterns are no more than what each of us is.

What is interesting and challenging is that on any given day, each fire station in America takes on the personality of the crew that resides there. If a certain crew consists of mostly positive people who are motivated and have good leadership, that particular station on that particular day, through its crew, will reflect a similar demeanor. The next day, the opposite may be the case, and since most departments have three shifts, A, B, and C, each day will usually be different from the day before in terms of personality, or family atmosphere.

"A" shift works as a cohesive unit that enjoys each other's company, loves to train and work on projects, works out and eats together, and has a captain who is positive, complimentary, participates in the less than glamorous assignments, and cooks for the crew at least once each cycle. This crew finishes its work on time, has a good rapport with the public, is productive, and has fun at work. Needless to say, the time goes by pretty fast for this crew, and it always looks forward to coming back from days off. The house rocks with laughter when this group is on duty.

A taskmaster who accomplishes goals by barking orders and making threats of additional work and other punishments if objectives are not met within a rigid time frame runs "B" shift. He or she generally acts the fool, but is always right. Just ask. The captain demands respect by using and forcing rank and words to the effect of "because I'm in charge and I said so" as responses to questions regarding working conditions. As the "quarterback," he or she often fumbles the snap and the team carries itself as if it was on a twelve-game losing streak. All the players are looking to be traded.

"C" shift may be somewhat dysfunctional, with a captain who lacks discipline and motivation, and encourages his or her brothers and sisters to behave the same. The personality of the station when this family is present will be anything but positive, presenting morale problems for those who are motivated and attempting to remain upbeat.

The strange and nice thing about the fire service is that

once 911 is dialed by someone and the bell rings, personality quirks disappear and each body is taken over by a spirit that only wants to do good, and that is what the public sees. We can go back to being silly later.

Life, as described in the fire service, reflects life at home. Just as different fire department structures contain their own types of families with A, B, and C shifts, traditional and contemporary family units have their own versions, along with D, E, F and X, Y and Z. The personalities of the children and adults that are associated with each letter reflect the structure of that particular unit.

The spirit that brought the fire crews together when the bell rang could be the same spirit that brings a family together. In the middle of a heated argument among the adults, one of the children appears, crying because the dog got out and is missing. In an instant the argument is over and the search is on for the dog, which happens to be found and rescued two hours later after combing the neighborhood and surrounding areas.

An efficient and well-conditioned fire crew is very much like a strong family. Although there may be individuals who present challenges to the team, each member possesses good qualities and is capable of making contributions to its betterment. Those qualities may be quite evident and easily accessed, or perhaps the team leaders (mothers, fathers, chiefs, captains, big brothers, and sisters) need to utilize their own skills and qualities in order to effectively bring out the best in certain family members.

The qualities that help meld a team are the same qualities that will help any family or family-type structure become better, healthier, and happier. The efforts that we make toward building a solid team can also be directed towards developing ourselves into better, healthier, and happier individuals.

# 2

# Life's Choices and Baseball

From the moment we enter the world, there are events that take place which help to mold us into the people we become. As children, we are most influenced by adults, our parents, teachers, grandparents, aunts and uncles, and other people we are close to and look up to. However, we reach a point where the people we become are the result of our own doing, through our own choices, like it or not. People influence us in either a good or a bad way, but the responsibilities for the decisions we make and our responses to that influence are totally ours, especially as adults. We may put blame on others because we turned out to be selfish, angry, egotistical, or miserable, but we had a choice. If we turn out to be compassionate and happy, there was probably a good deal of influence from positive role models, but it was our choice to recognize that influence and become this way.

Life can be seen sometimes as a journey, with a beginning and an end. What happens in between are the days, and a good day is such not because there weren't any bumps in the road or we didn't have a flat tire or the car didn't break down. A good day happens because we met and conquered the challenges of the day. We should know that the day isn't perfect, but there are twenty-four hours there for us to get something good out of it, and often all it takes is a moment to make it a great one, for us and for others. Too many times it seems that truly insignificant moments ruin the day for too many people.

Life can also be seen as a game and is often referred to by many as the "game of life." A game is supposed to be fun, so we'll take it a bit further and look at it as the "baseball game of life."

Baseball is the only game in which every person in the ballpark has a role and is, directly or indirectly, a part of the game and also a part of its history and tradition. The players, coaches, managers, and umpires are directly involved in the game. The fans, vendors, public address announcer, groundskeepers, and broadcasters, though indirectly involved, provide the majority of the charisma that makes the game so special.

Our day is a lot like a baseball game. Depending on our role in a particular moment or segment of time, we can be a player as part of an entire team, or a spectator. Our day always requires some type of teamwork in order to accomplish objectives, be it at home, at work, or out in public. We may be the manager of the team at home and a player at work. In public, we may make an assist by opening a door for someone with two arms full of groceries. That won't show up in the box score, but the teamwork we exhibited kept the momentum going and made that day a winner.

Statistics and numbers are very important to the individual ball player. The higher the batting average, the better, and the lower the earned run average, the better. However, how the team performs as a unit determines its place in the standings. Our individual stats on a particular day may not be so great, but we can still make contributions to the team and come out with a win. We might have gone zero for four at the plate, but the diving catch we made in the outfield and the sacrifice bunt that put the winning run in scoring position did as much to help the team win as the player who went four for four.

The words "I" and "me" are the most overused words in the English language and sound pretty dumb when coming out of the same mouth for any considerable length of time (they are seldom used in this book). The team player doesn't feel the need to use these words too often because they represent selfishness, isolation, and desperation. Though it's great to like ourselves, nobody ever makes it alone. Our greatness is only justified by our sincere recognition and appreciation of those who made the effort and devoted the time to give us good direction, thus subconsciously proving their own greatness and unselfishness as well.

Our attitude and response to what we are exposed to is what we are, by choice. A reasonable person realizes and accepts the fact that life is not always fair, and never perfect. Yet that person will strive to be the best he or she is decently capable of being, without compromise. If our efforts fall short of our desires and we have no control over the results, we will accept the hand we are dealt and not make excuses. We realize there are other opportunities in other things, perhaps things that are more worthwhile than what we had pursued before.

Though life can be looked at as a journey or a game, it is foremost a gift. Those fortunate enough to see it as such appreciate each day, perhaps in different ways, but with the same basic approach. As each batter in baseball has a different stance, all successful hitters will have the same approach when it is time to hit the pitch. That approach includes stepping toward the ball, staying focused on the pitch, keeping the hands in a position to generate maximum bat speed and power, staying in control of the swing, and following through.

Life throws us pitches all the time with fastballs, change-ups, and a lot of curves. The pitchers we face are the people we come in contact with every day, such as family members, friends, work associates, casual acquaintances, and strangers. They are people who support us and challenge us, and each pitch they throw us challenges us to respond. Our response is our swing, and our approach to how well we swing is our attitude. A good approach to life's pitches will result in a controlled, yet powerful swing, consistent, solid contact and a complete follow-through. If we miss a pitch, we just get back in the box and have another whack at the next one.

As a pitch in baseball requires split-second response, a pitch in life can have responses that last anywhere from seconds to years, even a lifetime. If we are not making the kind of contact that produces the results we want, it's up to us to change our approach, our attitude, which in turn changes our swing, hopefully for the better. The pitchers are not going to change, that's a guarantee. In life, that job belongs to the batter, and whereas in baseball a successful batter gets a hit thirty percent of the time, in life that's not good enough.

So what do all of these baseball comparisons mean when we translate them to the base hits we are trying to get in life? They mean it's tough to get a hit in life, even with a good approach or attitude. The pitchers in life are a lot tougher than any pitcher on the mound, even the all-stars. They will throw some nasty stuff at us, such as driving through an intersection in front of us when we have the right of way, or not saying "thank you" when we do something nice for them. They will be mean to us when we didn't do anything to them, and lie, degrade, physically abuse, and take us for granted. They will also use us and try to manipulate us. These pitches just described are the change-ups, curves, knuckleballs, sliders, and screwballs. They are really tough to hit because they are not always in the strike zone, and it's better if we don't respond to them, or swing.

Batting .300 in life is not going to make it for us. We have to bat as close to 1,000 (one thousand) as our approach and attitude will allow us to. What's great about life's baseball games is that when we don't swing at certain pitches, we still get a hit. If the only thought we give that inconsiderate driver is that an accident didn't happen, then we connected for a solid single. If we acknowledge that the reason people can't respond to kindness or are mean is because they have problems and are unhappy, that's a double in the alley. We don't believe the lies but do believe we are good, *boom!* a triple off of the top of the wall! They attempt to discount, hurt, use, and abuse us, and we walk away? They've just lost the best friend they ever had, *crack! a grand slam!*

We'll always have these nasty pitches thrown at us; the curves, sliders, changes, and other off speed stuff designed to fool us. However, as long as we don't swing at them, our lifetime batting average will continue to climb. We would have never known who Babe Ruth was had he consistently tried to hit them, which takes us to the fastball down the middle.

This pitch is the best one to hit, the one we should swing at. We won't see it very often in a game, but when we do, we need to be ready for it because it's the one we can hit the hardest and be the most productive with. In life, this is the pitch we should go after, for this is the pitch of love, kindness, compassion, laughter, goodness, support, and friendship.

A good hitter will be patient and wait for a good pitch to hit. Luckily, in the game of life, we get more than three strikes, and as long as we have heartbeats and breaths, we have at-bats. The key is to respond to the good pitches and to lay off the bad ones. Not only will we hit them, but we'll learn to throw them as well.

# 3

# Inspiration through Older Folks
# and Kids

As firefighters, we are able to see a lot of things that affect us in different ways. The situations we find ourselves in always involve people in need of assistance in one way or another. At times, these situations stir our emotions, but we try to learn and grow from them. The events are often tragic, but once in a while a comedy results. The people we are trying to help are exhibiting, either way, a great deal of courage. In the heat of the moment, they don't realize how much they are helping us and how inspired some of us are becoming. They may never realize it, but the inspiration we gain can be everlasting.

Cases involving serious trauma or illness usually leave us with memories that may take a long time to get over. Rarely are they forgotten, but in special instances we are able to gain inspiration from a patient or victim that offers us more than just awareness of our mortality. We are provided with new and better ways to appreciate life's true treasures. These blessings give us opportunities to experience things that can actually mold us and provide direction, perhaps even change our attitude and approach in the "baseball game of life."

It seems that the greatest emotional experiences we encounter are in those situations involving children or elderly people. No matter how bad things may seem, these ageless little people and grownups refuse to allow the circumstances to set them back. One of our crew's most memorable encounters of this sort, in a lighter tone, was when we responded to the aid of a ninety-year-old woman who had injured her hip and fallen to the ground. When we arrived at her home, she had already managed to get herself onto her bed and was sitting there waiting for us as we entered the house. To say her left hip appeared to be dislocated is a gross understatement, for we could tell just by looking at it with her clothes still on. It looked as if she had a grapefruit in her pants where her hip was supposed to be, perhaps the worst dislocation we had ever seen. Yet this courageous woman, two days after her ninetieth birthday, just sat there smiling, happy to see us. She was totally coherent with not even a grimace of pain as we moved her from her house to the ambulance. At one point while transporting her to the hospital, we asked her how she was feeling. She responded, "It's starting to get a little sore." This magnificent human work of art was the talk of the station for a large piece of the shift. The inspiration she showered upon us was monumental as we all talked about the lady's courage and determination not to let this injury get her down.

Older people are often discounted by narrow- and shallow-minded types of all ages as being unwilling and unable to accomplish objectives, perform tasks, fulfill dreams, or even function. These same people feel that once they themselves arrive at this juncture that they so despise, the same should automatically happen to them. It seems that a lot of us convince ourselves at an early age to realize this goal without so much as a fight.

In the fire service, we always tell ourselves, "never give up!" We face physical, mental, and emotional challenges every day, and we have to meet and conquer them, or at least try. Our approach and attitude play a big part in whether or not we are successful, so it's best to be in the right frame of mind. Most of the time it helps. At times, the odds are very much against us and losing the battle is imminent, but the quality of the efforts made can minimize casualties. A sincere and valiant effort resulting at some point in defeat is victory nonetheless.

There are no guarantees or promises in life except for the consequences of not trying. Those of us who succumb to the beliefs that life's rewards are meant only for the physically young have foolishly and subconsciously given up. To believe this is to make us old before our time, whether we are a child or an adult. It is a curse we put upon ourselves, a prison sentence that we begin to serve the minute we believe it, and if we turn our backs on the inspirational gifts of our elders, there is no possibility for parole.

Every day these gifts are offered to us in so many ways, and hopefully we are able to recognize, accept, and appreciate them. The early morning jogger, the college student, the actor, singer and dancer in the local play, the police officer, the firefighter, the volunteer high school baseball coach; the swimmer, the writer, the teacher we had who is teaching our children are all proud of what they continue to achieve and earn, along with our respect and gratitude.

At the gym where our shift works out, a woman is there in a wheelchair every day. She wheels herself to each station, pulls herself out of the chair, does her exercises, puts herself back into the chair and moves on to the next station. To us she is the strongest woman in the world, with character to match.

How much inspiration will it take for us to actually do the things we aspire to at the age we're not supposed to? Do we have any idea of what it will take to accomplish the things we are witnessing in the people we hope are our pre-decessors? Do we have control over our attitude, and does mind over matter really matter? All we can do is have faith that the foundation we have laid for ourselves is solid and the journey we have put ourselves on has good direction. The combination can provide a healthy outlook for the future, should we be so fortunate to make it there.

So, as careful children, when told to respect our elders, listen, for we may very well be protecting ourselves and the quality of our future. If we get the chance, we need to find shelter under the wing of someone older, a lot older, who has the wisdom of many years, but the heart and spirit of a child. There is so much we can learn about perspective, reality, inner strength, and remaining young at heart or growing young. Remember, as long as we breathe, growing older is mandatory, but getting old is an option.

Just as older people offer us the opportunity to a better attitude and approach, so do children, as they provide us with plenty of chances to not take ourselves too seriously. They speak only the truth because that is all they know at this juncture, and no matter how it comes out, somewhere there is a message. Often the message is just the smile they put on our faces, but every now and then, they'll come up with something that will make us take a good hard look at ourselves. They have the ability to offer us perspective and awareness, perhaps more subtly than our elders, but just as effectively. The key for us is to listen to what our children have to say and not discount their ability to teach us as well. We need to get close to and talk to them from the minute they are born, and understand that as they grow, they may feel the need to break away from us at some point. This can happen in different ways, physically, socially, or emotionally, but we need to maintain a balance of flexibility and discipline and allow it to happen. If done right, they will always come back to us and we will always be there. This may not make a difference in their needing us, but it will in their wanting us. Our children are a valuable part of our own growth, and we will need and want them as well, so the fewer barriers on both sides, the better.

In our lives as firefighters, we have seen displays of tremendous courage from children that have changed our lives. Any of us in all walks of life would be hard pressed not to gain appreciation for our blessings were we to witness the same.

Danny, the nephew of one of our captains, was diagnosed with neuroblastoma, a cancer of the central nervous system, in 1993, at the age of two. He was given almost no chance of surviving the illness as he went through what seemed like countless battles and treatments. Among them were chemotherapy, surgery, radiation treatments, a bone marrow transplant, and one year of isolation. He also experienced cardiac arrest on the operating table. Danny's grandfather, our captain's father, also had cancer during this time and died in August of 1993, ending another battle in a period of devastation that might have destroyed a lot of families. However, the family got through this amazing time, in large part due to the attitudes and approaches of Danny and his grandfather.

These courageous men, generations apart in physical age, never allowed the disease to weaken their spirits and their determination to beat it. They provided the family with opportunities for significant personal growth and experiences along with tremendous inspiration and appreciation for daily blessings. The love that the family provided helped Danny's grandfather fight back at the disease and for Danny and his immediate family, conquer it. On Thanksgiving of 1999, Danny was deemed cancer-free.

Another touching story is that of Jessica, the daughter

of one of our battalion chiefs, who at age one was so conditioned to her treatment sessions that as soon as the nurse entered her room, she would reach her hands out, palms up. This was to allow the nurse to begin the painful treatment and therapy on the second- and third-degree burns she had on her hands as the result of an accident.

Firefighters in our area volunteer their spare time to drive children who have cancer, and their parents, to hospitals and centers where they can receive their treatments. We are also involved in support systems for children who are being treated in burn centers and help raise donations for a local charity for children with life-threatening diseases. To only have our hearts broken by these experiences is to prove how selfish we are, but to honor these little troopers by becoming better people is to raise ourselves to their level. The only things about these kids that are different are that their smiles are brighter, their laughter is louder, and their focus is keener. Their courage and inspiration are contagious to the point where we can't help but exhibit some of the symptoms we have been exposed to.

A lot of these kids will never have the chance to grow older and pass their wisdom onto younger generations, but they have done it for older generations. They have already inspired so many in such a short time, leaving lasting impressions that can mold and shape lives for the better. They are heroes to all of us, and those of us with enough sense to see this can make good things happen inside ourselves, which in turn will allow us to do the same for others.

# 4

# Brother Jones

In chapter 3, we encouraged people to embrace the wisdom of an older person, one who is young at heart and growing younger. For many people, this may be easier said than done, sort of like looking for true love. However, some of us are blessed with the good fortune of having someone come into our lives, completely unexpected, and touching us in a way that we will never again be the same.

For some reason, our fire department was lucky enough to have Mr. Talmadge Jones enter our lives this way in a food booth at the 1999 Blues Festival in Monterey. A friend of ours, Pat (Lyin' Pat) DuVal, a former Monterey County sheriff's deputy, worked with us, and was the one who asked Jones to help us. In the three long days and nights that we spent working together, we all had the opportunity to become acquainted with Jones, and we all fell in love with him. In spite of the difficult hours, which passed by quickly, we shared more laughter than people are supposed to when working that hard. By the end of the festival, we all felt as if we had known him all of our lives. Jones is the fondest memory any of us has of the festival, though not a distant one, as we have stayed in touch and become very close to him. We have made him an honorary member of our fire department, and he checks up on us quite often.

We have learned so much from and about this unusual man born July 18, 1929. Our relationship started in front of a barbecue pit and has grown and developed ever since. The first thing we learned about Jones was his tremendous sense of humor. Not a day has passed being with him that didn't contain at least one hearty belly laugh, the kind that makes you feel as if your stomach is going to burst. Laughter is our foundation that helps us get by in day-to-day living and dealing with people. It also keeps us from taking ourselves too seriously, something most of us could do less of. For example, on a really busy and tough day at work, if you were to ask Jones how it's going, he'll say, "Man, I don't know whether to shit or go blind, so I'm just gonna close my eyes and fart!" Another response might be, "I feel like I've been through hell wearing gasoline drawers!" On a really good day, he'll say, "I'm shittin' in high cotton and wiping my ass with the bolls!" Even the most prudent individual would have a hard time being offended by the "tasteful" profanity that Jones sprinkles into the conversation. To truly appreciate the poetic flair that turns bad words rosy, one has to hear it in person, but Jones would never talk this way in front of someone he wasn't sure would not be offended. He's a gentleman's gentleman and a master of discretion.

To only know the funny side of Jones is to order a seven-course meal, taste the appetizers, and then go home without the doggy bag. The wisdom, passion, kindness, patience, love and trust he feels that we have earned from him make us feel so privileged and honored. We feel especially privileged to have been able to hear about all the experiences that make up Jones's life. He has told us of his adventures as a child growing up in North Carolina and his relationships with his parents, grandparents, aunts, uncles, cousins, and friends. He's shared with us his life on the railroad, his proud career in the United States Army and his work and relationships with the inmates at the county jail.

As a child, Jones was no different from any other energetic boy, getting into mischief at home and at school. One day, he knew he was going to get a "whuppin'," so he put on five pairs of pants. When the time came, his mother said to him, "Pull 'em all off, son. Today it's pure ass!" At school, Jones got a whuppin' from his teacher, who then gave him a note to his mother telling her what had happened. When his mother read the note, she gave him another whuppin', wrote "thank you," on the note she received, and had him give the note back to the teacher. Jones once said that if child abuse were an issue when he was young the way it is today, his mother would have been put on death row. When she really got mad at him, she would say, "I'm gonna squeeze something out of you that looks like potatoes!"

All the whuppins that Jones joked about didn't seem to bother him that much, because he turned out pretty good, and very wise. He has many sayings about life that contain few words, but speak volumes. His advice to children, "No cards, no knife, no dice" and "You don't have to break the rules to be cool." His advice to everyone is, "To love people, you have to love yourself" and "Keep a cool head and a clear thought."

This next passage is something Jones read to us one day, which is something we can all live by. "A person can be worthwhile and deserving. I love myself the way I am for my life to be fulfilled. Program yourself to believe in yourself and stay motivated. See the big picture, be forward, and chart your own course. Don't let anyone else control your destiny, and set yourself your own goal."

Jones is certainly one of a kind, and to have him in our lives has truly been a rare experience and a blessing. We often wonder, "Why us?" He is a teacher, philosopher, humanitarian, philanthropist, comedian, poet, the best barbecuer in the world (if you were to ask how good, he would tell you, "I can barbecue water"), and to us an ageless friend and spirit. His words whenever we part company as he heads home or to the barbershop to tell or hear a "lie" are, "Be cool and always be kind to your neighbor."

Sometimes I feel that people take advantage of Jones's good nature without showing appreciation. When I bring it up to him, his response is, "That's the price of sweetness." The world would surely be a better place if his spirit lived in all of us.

# 5

# Anatomy Class

Our class is basic and simple, concentrating on the eyes, ears, mouth, brain, the functions of the hands, and the best use of our legs and feet.

Some questions come to mind immediately, such as, why do we have two ears but only one mouth? Do our hands work best when holding on or letting go, and do we notice that when we point a finger, there are three fingers pointing back? Do our legs and feet function better by moving forward or being in reverse and moving backward? Is our eyesight sharper looking ahead, and is there risk of a neck injury by constantly looking back?

A lot of us do not use our ears to the best of our abilities for some interesting reasons. Many of us in positions as leaders (we are all in these positions at some time during the day, if only for a moment) or perceived positions of power, either at home or at work, seem to think that our positions or rank automatically qualify us as an authority. We somehow "lose sight of our hearing" and choose not to listen just because we're The Boss. At the same time we talk too much and don't communicate, or talk too little and don't communicate.

As leaders, or the bosses at home (parents and guardians), we too often discount our children by either ignoring them and not being involved in their lives in a constructive way, or by being overbearing and bossy and not allowing them to make the decisions they're capable of making. We have enough interest in them to tell them what to do, but not to listen to what they have to say. Their opinions and observations do count, and we can learn from them as well, sometimes better than we can teach. It's a matter of being willing to listen enough to show we are a real leader, and not just The Boss.

When we observe certain types of behavior (symptoms) in our children at home or our so-called subordinates at work that appear inappropriate but are the result of being triggered, how do we respond? Are we The Boss and simply tell them to stop, or are we a leader and ask what the problem (cause) is? The longer we don't show interest in, or address the cause, the longer the symptoms will continue and the worse they will become. Behavior, whether from children or adults, that starts out as an attempt at getting attention and is ignored will at some point be motivated by spite and blind disrespect. As leaders, we can prevent situations from reaching this point by using our mouths and ears to the best of our abilities, which hopefully helped us to earn the position we are in.

At home, are we just a disciplinarian, or do we challenge ourselves to teach our children what is right, treat them with respect and fairness, and then have the courage to loosen the reins when they should be loosened? At work, do we crack the whip for eight hours and accomplish nothing, or do we listen to our troops tell us what needs to be done and empower them with the ownership and responsibility needed to accomplish the objective and realize the goal? Do we, the troops, speak to our leaders in a tone that will encourage them to listen? Do we appreciate the efforts that are made and say so, whether it is at work with our colleagues or at home with our kids and spouses? This is a good time to use the mouth constructively because the ears have hopefully already done their job.

Our eyes are perhaps the trickiest part of our anatomy. We see some things clearly, yet others not so. A lot of times the hardest thing for any of us to see is the goodness in ourselves. The easiest thing to see is the goodness of others or their apparent goodness on the surface. As children, we may be easily convinced that there is not much worth in us, either by convincing ourselves or from being convinced by others. Those who are unable to use their own ears and mouths effectively usually do this to their children. At this stage of our lives, our ears are not being used effectively as well, but only because they have not yet fully developed. The result may be low self-esteem, and as much as we wish it would not be, we allow negativity a lot of power, not realizing at this point in our lives there is positive feedback as well, from ourselves as well as others. We may hear positive things directed at us, but for some reason, we don't give it the credence that we do the negative. We don't believe our ears.

We are allowed a certain amount of slack as children, and the environment we are in or put ourselves in influences us greatly into how we see ourselves. We don't really have a choice at this stage, and a lot has to do with what we have been hearing from others and believing. We may look in the mirror and see something that we think is bad, resulting in a low opinion of ourselves. On the other hand, we may see something that we think is good, but really isn't, thus producing arrogance. At some point, hopefully soon, we correct our vision and never look backwards with the same frequency. When this happens, our neck does not hurt so much from the strain of constantly looking back to where we have been.

As adults we have to realize that yes, perhaps something happened to us as children that created a lot of stuff in us ("my father" this, "my mother" that). However, now it's up to us to maintain the goodness that was instilled in us as a child, or instill it into ourselves if that wasn't the case. There are no excuses now, only choices. We can now take an honest look in the mirror and give validity to the truth by liking and accepting what we see or by doing something about what we don't like. The criticism of ourselves and of others can give way to compassion, and we no longer have to be afraid to be kind, or afraid, period. We can see the true goodness in ourselves and the true goodness in others.

Improving our vision seems to improve other parts of our anatomy. It enables us to be able to operate our hands to their fullest potential. We learn to hold onto only that which is worth holding, and when we point to a problem we see three fingers pointing back suggesting we be a part of the solution. The compassion and fearlessness we have from clear vision allows us to hold onto those things in our lives that are good for us and to let go of the negative things that we have no control over and are no longer valid excuses. So much time and energy is wasted here, and since we never know how much time we have, why not use it effectively and be productive and positive with it? We dreamed of playing in the majors and worked hard to get there, gave it our best shot, but for some reason, it just didn't happen. We can blame a lot of things for why it didn't work out, or we can say we just weren't good enough and the effort was all that mattered.

At this point, or fairly soon afterward, we hopefully realize there are other, probably more important things we can now do. The same effort, passion, and desire can be put into becoming a teacher, firefighter, doctor, police officer, writer, or anything else we may aspire to. A goal not realized, when looked upon with clear vision, is not a failure, but an opportunity to do something else that may very well be better than before. We are by no means limited to only one dream, which brings us to the following story.

When I was a volunteer firefighter, I ran my first cardiac arrest save with Brian McEldowney, my good friend since childhood and one of my fire department crew mates on this call. Brian and I played baseball together for many years, through Little League, Pony League, Babe Ruth League, Connie Mack League, high school, and semi-pro. Our paths separated when we chose different colleges to attend. He was one of the best pitchers ever to come out of this area, and I looked to him as a big brother. I still feel this way about him.

If you haven't by now figured out who the person in this book is with the passion for baseball, it's me. I'm also the guy who dreamed about playing pro ball, and since you probably have never heard of me, you know it didn't happen, but that's not important. However, I was considered the complete package, bursting with talent. I had deceptive speed, a lot slower than I looked, and although I couldn't move too well I made up for it by being clumsy.

On this particular night with the fire department, I don't remember what year, but it was the night before Easter, I was in charge of patient care. The man we responded to had no heartbeat and was not breathing. We performed cardiopulmonary resuscitation (CPR) on him, and I also delivered electrical shocks with the defibrillator. By the time we arrived at the hospital, the man's heartbeat and breathing had been restored, the result of a great team effort and the will of a higher power than us. He continued his life as before, normal and happy.

Brian gave me far too much credit for what took place that night. He was also aware of how disappointed I was when my baseball dream didn't come true. As we were putting the ambulance back in service at the hospital, Brian said something to me that, at that moment, put my life in balanced perspective for the first time in a long time. He said, "That's better than any home run you ever hit!" I never felt the same about baseball or the fire service again.

Good vision gets us going in the right direction, and this is where our feet and legs come into play. We've all been asked at some point, some more than others, "Why don't you watch where you are going?" This usually happens when we lose focus on what is ahead of us. We are usually looking in a direction other than where we are heading, or intend to be heading. Too often we are looking back, and when this happens, our feet lose direction and we start bumping into things. The pain we get in our neck is from always looking back, and as long as our neck is twisted and our vision blurred, our feet cannot function, our legs are useless, and we'll keep stumbling. The pain we feel in our necks from the strain of the constant head swivel is the same pain we feel in our hearts from our swiveling minds and thoughts to the past and what could have been. What has happened cannot be changed, and disappointments happen every day, but remember, life is a journey and a game. Tomorrow will bring other opportunities, maybe greater than the ones we were dreaming about, but there **will be** more opportunities. Our previous career or ambition ended before we reached the goal attached to our dreams, and our journey had a stretch of rough road that threw us off course. In the entire scheme of things, these types of events affect only us and do not alter the world as much as we would like them to. It doesn't mean the game is over and the journey has ended, because hopefully there is reasonable time to grieve, recover, and move forward. As long as we have tomorrows, there is always something to look forward to.

When this is our approach, our vision will be clear and our head straight, our feet will get back on track, our legs will move in the right direction, our hands will know when to let go, and the pain will go away. The proper use of our ears will allow us to listen to everyone and everything worth listening to and not restrict ourselves to certain age or employee groups or perceived hierarchies. If we've made good use of our two ears, our one mouth will do a better job of speaking and we will no longer seem so noisy.

It's great to have tomorrows and hopefully we will have lots of them, because they give us the opportunities to take lessons, learn from, and respond to those lessons. Remember, those of us that need reminding, we never know how long we will be here. The mere knowledge of mortality is not enough for most of us to value what we have, or to be the best we can be from within and live a happy life. It seems that we need to be hit over the head, again and again, reminded by tragedy that life is too short for us to be stuck in ways that are not good. With each kick in the head, we promise ourselves, and others, we will do better. Too often the efforts are not sincere or are short-lived, and we go back to our old ways until the next reminder, or until we become a reminder for someone else. Understanding the critical parts of our anatomy and allowing those different body parts to function most effectively will save us a lot of heartaches.

# 6

# Feed and Water Your Relationships

"No one cares how much you know until they know how much you care." This is a quote from an instructor who taught a leadership class that our crew attended. It says so much and applies to every situation imaginable where people have to team up to make good things happen. It is a simple, common sense idea that will help maintain and strengthen any relationship, be it personal, professional, or among strangers. Statements and attitudes such as "be nice" and "egos eat brains," when applied with the right approach, can produce enjoyable environments and eliminate obstacles to allow goals to be realized without compromise or personal sacrifice.

It seems easy enough to recognize the things we need to do to strengthen or maintain our relationships, and being nice is always a good start and a good choice. It can be risky, and at times requires all of the courage in the world. There is always a chance that being nice to people, even the people we are close to, will end up hurting us. However, sincere kindness sets us free from fear and we can take the risks that come with being nice without worrying about it. Those of us who are not afraid are not concerned if someone is not nice to us in return, whether it is those close to us or total strangers. We know there is a chance this may happen, but it's not our problem. There are a lot of people who are afraid to be nice and we cannot change that. It's best not to worry about it, because if we do, it becomes our problem as well. Those whom we don't know that treat people badly, we shouldn't worry about at all. It's best that we don't know them and are not close to them. Those whom we are close to and know well can possibly be afforded some patience, but only to a certain point. If we spend years being nice to people who are incapable of responding accordingly, then we must make some adjustments. We don't necessarily have to be unkind, just different, perhaps giving them not as much of ourselves and our time.

Feeding our relationships can be done literally. At the firehouse, the most enjoyable part of the day for our crew is when we are gathered in the kitchen. We like this time and try to have at least one meal together on shift.

Take a group of total strangers and gather them amongst good food. There is no doubt that when they partake in the offerings, conversation will begin to flow, laughter will surface, and it will seem automatic that everyone will begin to have a good time. There is really no need for anything else; no music, television, games, or even a theme. Good food and people produce good times and good communication, and this is why we eat together at work. It's a good opportunity to learn more about each other and get to know each other better, find out what kind of a day it's been for everyone, and to simply grow as a team or a family. This is a good way for all families to spend a part of the day together, and it doesn't even require as much of an effort as one might think.

A lot of people don't have the desire to cook, feel they don't have the time, or may think something such as this is not necessary. If we are truly interested in keeping our relationships strong, this is certainly worth a try, so just get some good, healthy food. In the time it takes to boil a pot of water, we can whip up a tasty pasta sauce or at least heat up a jar of good quality prepared stuff. Still don't want to cook? Okay, then try going to just about any grocery store and find a nice variety of hot entrees and side dishes that are tasty and nutritious. Independent stores and small chains usually have the best in terms of quality. Take it from us, firefighters know where to get the best food.

When our relationships with our spouses or significant others began, we probably went out to eat or cooked for each other often. We got to know each other during this time, but maybe weren't quite aware of its purpose. This was a time for impressions and courtship, and we always seemed to have a good time when it was just the food and us. Hopefully this has carried on over time, with courting still a part of it, but just talking about the day and learning more about each other replacing attempts to impress. No matter how much time we spend together, we should still go on dates (with each other), and they don't have to be extravagant. Sharing a snack or a meal will almost certainly be a compliment, with the right attitude.

This is also a good thing to do with our children from the time they are born. Cook for them, eat with them, and ask how things are going at school with their studies, friends, and teachers. Help them realize, without forcing it, that home is a good place to be, a good place to bring friends, to eat, spend time, and have fun. Show them Mom and Dad are cool, not because we're competing, but because we've always been this way, and when we help the kids with the dishes, man we're really cool! Good company and good food are a good combination.

There are other ways to feed and water our relationships in addition to the meal table. We are reminded that we have to "work at our relationships," but perhaps it's better that we play at them. It starts with liking ourselves enough to like the people we are close to. Our buddy Jones always tells us "to love others we have to love ourselves." This needs to be our approach and attitude to so many things, if not everything. This also helps us tolerate those we come in contact with that we aren't close to, who come and go on a daily basis and shouldn't affect our days or lives significantly, as a rule. If there is a major impact from these people, it is hopefully something positive.

When our relationships need feeding, it's because, for some reason, we have stopped doing the things that were causing them to grow and strengthen in the first place. We spend time and play with our children when they are tiny, so why not continue to play with them as they grow and after they have grown? We can show the same interest in our children's adult activities as we did in their childhood activities. We can still shoot baskets, go to movies and ball games, or otherwise set aside some time designated for each other. Call it dates with our kids. It's just as much fun to do these things when we are all adults, perhaps even more so, since our kids can sometimes treat and we don't need to go with them to the restroom every twenty minutes. Doing these things and letting go of the inhibitions that suggest we shouldn't do them are all it takes. Talking to our grown children about their work, family, and what interests them now will help continue to grow blossoms in our relationships with them, and theirs with us. Letting them know that when we go our separate ways or time does not allow these activities as regularly as we might wish, there is still the desire to have the same fun again when the opportunity rises. That desire is based upon how we feel for each other and not on what we want to do. So if certain things are not possible because of time, geographic or physical restrictions, our feelings for each other can continue to be strong because of the solid foundation we built a long time ago. The mutual caring and things we do together help feed and water our relationships, and this is what keeps them alive.

We all possess the so-called "child within" us, something that a lot of us do not let out for others to experience, especially ourselves. The child within us is a great tool for feeding and watering our relationships, because it is pure and innocent, uninhibited and free. It is especially good for the relationships we have with ourselves.

Inside an adult, the child does not care what others think, because it is having fun, not hurting anyone, and hopefully not misbehaving. It likes to spend time with both children and adults, and guys like Sylvester, Yosemite Sam, Foghorn Leghorn, Tweety Bird, the Dover Boys, Tom and Jerry, and Wile E. Coyote (Super Genius). For those of us who know who these characters are, the very thought of them will most likely bring a smile, for they are friends to generations of children, both growing and grown.

Our crew at the firehouse wakes up each morning to the television turned on to Looney Tunes and the creations of Chuck Jones, Fritz Freleng, Carl Stalling, Mel Blanc, and the rest of the team at Warner Brothers who touched so many of our lives. Not everyone at the firehouse will sit and watch, but if only for a moment, those who do always get a chuckle out of it or remember a particular episode from years ago. It's all part of the child within us coming out to play. If others want to play, they are welcomed, but if they don't, we won't try and force them, because we are too busy having fun.

The child within is different for all of us, but we all have things that we like and are comfortable with that relate to our childhood. The problem seems to be that too many of us are afraid to let the child surface because we think that being grown up prohibits it. We are too often concerned about what other people will think of our "childlike" behavior to allow it to happen. A big part of being a child is not having the inhibitions that prevent some of us from being as free with our spirit as we would like to be. As responsible adults wishing to be children from time to time, we have the ability to monitor our behavior to our liking while at the same time not being destructive toward, or disrespectful of others, at least in theory. If we are watching cartoons, playing with dolls, having a sleepover with our nieces and nephews, cuddling with our pets, making milkshakes, or just hanging out with kids, it shouldn't be a problem for anyone else. It's no fun being an adult unless you can act like a kid.

If our relationships are dying, it's because we are killing them. Just as the flowers in our gardens need feeding and watering to flourish and avoid being droopy, so do our relationships with kindness, affection, attention, a child's spirit, and a well-stocked refrigerator. For those of us who remember or happen to notice on the reruns, that's the first place Wally and Beaver headed for when they came home from school every day. Mrs. Cleaver certainly knew what she was doing with those great-looking sandwiches and wholesome, well-balanced meals she made, along with bowls of fruit and freshly baked cake with frosting and ice-cold milk. With a little bit of extra effort from herself and Ward, everything else seemed to fall into place. Problems didn't seem so big, Lumpy, Eddie Haskell, and Larry Mondello loved coming over, Mom and Dad ended up being "swell," and the boys turned out okay. As corny as some of that stuff was and is still perceived as such by many in the real world, it can definitely contribute a lot to the quality of our own personal and professional relationships.

# 7

# Positive Selfishness

So much has been emphasized about nurturing, strengthening, and maintaining the relationships we have with others, but what about the relationships we have with ourselves? There needs to be a balance between the two, with some people needing to devote more time to themselves while others need to be less self-serving.

It seems in today's society that too many people have a tendency to devote too much time and effort to themselves, and only themselves. It would seem that we all could get everything we ever wanted if we didn't care about the needs of others or how we went about it. A lot of people subscribe to this theory, believing that this is the only way to accomplish things and realize goals. Funny how there is a price to pay for getting what we want, and how expensive the price is depends a lot on the journey we take toward our goals. Do we act like the combination of a stampeding buffalo and a spoiled, screaming child to get our way, or are we considerate of others while in pursuit of a dream?

It has been proven time and time again that a sincere and decent effort does more and means more than an accomplishment obtained through behavior that is shady and questionable, lacking character and honor. This is just another corny statement that is laughed at by many until they receive the bill for their actions, making them believers. It's one of those buy now, pay later sort of things, and we never know when the due date is until it hits us in the face.

Caring about and putting others before us may be looked upon as foolish by a large segment of our society, but this type of approach is the stuff that heroes are made of. It does not come without its own price though if attention is not devoted to oneself to be able to charge one's batteries in order to keep on caring, without self-destructing. As those of us who do so know, caring for others can be very taxing and draining to the mind, body, and soul. We need an opportunity to care for ourselves as well, perhaps more opportunity than we seem to be willing to give ourselves on a regular basis. Just as we cannot love others until we can love ourselves, we cannot continue to be good to others if we are not good to ourselves.

Physical activity drains the body of energy, resulting in the need to nourish the body and replenish that energy. In the same sense, turning our attention to and caring for others on a consistent basis can drain our mind, spirit, and soul of their energy. How we replenish this energy can be different for just about everybody, but the energy and spirit have to be replenished or we will be no good for ourselves, and henceforth no good for anyone else. Just as we become light-headed, weak, and grumpy by not feeding our body when we should, we become tired, angry, and resentful by not feeding our mind, spirit, and soul in the same sense. As different as our nutritional diets are, so are our mental diets. Physical nourishment comes in the form of nutrients from the foods we eat, and mental nourishment can be whatever constructively suits the individual without harming others.

A good mental diet usually includes some form of physical activity that stimulates the heart and gets the blood flowing. For some, that could be working out at the gym, running, some sort of sports participation, or taking brisk walks. As a national standard, part of each shift at the firehouse is always set aside for physical fitness training, for this proves to be as stimulating for the mind and spirit as it is for the body. Other parts of a healthy mental diet might include some form of expression such as art, music, cooking, crafts, or writing. One of our firefighters composes music for his band, another is an excellent carpenter and craftsperson, and most of us are decent cooks. Meditation, yoga, and reading are also good ways to recharge, and don't forget to regularly bring that child inside all of us out to play. Finally, sometimes doing absolutely nothing can be the best thing any of us can do from time to time. We know some people who are seasoned pros at this and would be the healthiest people in the world if that were all it took. Those of us who live with cats can learn a lot from our furry friends by just observing how they spend the day. It usually involves eating, playing, sleeping, and not much else.

All of us at some time find ourselves, either at home or at work, in positions of trying to fulfill a seemingly never-ending list of one commitment after another. A good conditioning tool or attitude for those of us who seem to be labeled as "caretakers," unselfish, driven, ambitious, or just plain caring is to take occasional "times out." When we find ourselves being overwhelmed and the frustration, anger, and resentment start to surface, call time out and think of the best thing we could be doing at this exact moment, within reason. A time out in a ball game usually lasts a couple of minutes. What we are doing is probably more important than a game; so let's give ourselves a minimum of fifteen minutes, a little more if need be. In this amount of time we can go outside and get some air, take a quick walk, stretch ourselves, have a snack or a meal (we probably skip meals regularly), go for a short drive, pet the cat, or watch a cartoon (with the cat). With the amount of time we are spending on all those other things, which will be there anyway, we owe it to ourselves to recharge enough to help us through the tasks in a healthier manner. Later we can devote more time to ourselves or, if necessary, make the time. We have to in order to maintain our mental health, and for some of us, it can be a matter of mental and emotional survival.

In the fire and emergency services, disasters or situations with multiple casualties or demands require what is called "triage." The word *triage* is French for "to sort," which is what we need to do to determine who will receive our attention and service immediately and who will receive it on a delayed basis. The most urgent situations are dealt with right away, while other situations that can be in essence, put off until a better time, or until we are available, are handled in order of importance.

In the emergency field, we don't have the luxury of taking breaks during triage because we have to tend to each task as we come to it. However, triaging our own personal and working commitments does give us chances for times out, which can help get our heads back in the game. We will be better off and so will our friends, loved ones, and work mates.

# 8

# Teamwork

There is no "I" in "team," but there is an "M" and an "E," which spell "me."

On the fire ground or scene of a medical emergency or rescue operation, the worst thing that can happen to the crew is for one of its members to freelance. This is when a teammate goes off on his or her own and works independently of the group. This is usually done because freelancers think their ideas are better, or don't agree with the decisions being made by the person in charge. They also tend to be irresponsible, are not good listeners, and do not respect others, or themselves.

When firefighters do this, they are putting not only themselves, but also the entire team and the people we are trying to help at risk. "How could this be?" you might ask. "After all, you are firefighters and are not supposed to behave this way!" Let's just say it happens from time to time, and it is addressed. It is a thoughtless and selfish act that produces nothing good and can lead to disaster. It's because we are human, just another segment of society that has its own share of freelancers, to say the least.

Every day we are put in positions where we are required to work as a member of a team in order to accomplish objectives or just keep things flowing for ourselves and others. It happens at home, work, and in the general public and occurs in many situations, at times with people we don't even know. Remember in chapter 2, the one about life's choices and baseball and the inconsiderate driver that cut us off even though we had the right of way? This person was freelancing, not concerned about the rules of teamwork or the consequences that would affect him and the team, in this case, the other drivers who needed to pass through this intersection. If we are in this situation, do we act as a team player, approach the intersection with caution, and allow the other driver to pass, or are we freelancers as well and fight for what is ours? Maybe we can discuss the options with the firefighters and police as we are being loaded into the ambulance next to the other driver.

This is just one example of why teamwork is so important in all aspects of our lives. It certainly helps in our daily family life and at work, a necessity that contributes so much to the quality of all our relationships and acquaintances, when applied. However, it is too often discounted as most, if not all people who drive can attest to the previous example. Other examples come to mind as well, such as chores and duties that need to be done at home and at work, and whether or not they are shared or divided equitably. Are house duties divided between spouses and partners and between parents and children? This could go a long way when it comes time to talk to our kids about what they can say yes to and what they should say no to. Fire captains, if we clean a toilet in the station now and then, might that earn us a little respect from the crew that, when the time comes, will lay it all on the line when we're in a tough spot? Common, seemingly small courtesies extended to other people, whether we know them or not, are nothing less than acts of teamwork. That driver we just ran off the road might be the person conducting the job interview we are on our way to, and he or she got a really good look at us.

Selfishness is such a bad thing, totally counterproductive and destructive, plus it makes people kind of hate us. As bad as freelancing is, in comparison there is nothing better than experiencing and being a part of the coming together of a group to form a true team. Working together this way can help any situation in any organization.

# 9

# Workplace Relationships, Leadership, and Attitudes

During our working years, about one-fourth of our total time is spent on the job for those who work a forty-hour week. For a lot of us, much more of our time is spent on the job. When we discussed feeding and watering our relationships in chapter 6, it applied to *all* of our relationships. Whether we like it or not, we spend a lot of time with our colleagues at work. We are pretty much stuck with them, much the same as we are with our families. We don't really have a choice in the matter of whom we work with, so why not make the most of it? After all, these people are like family, our brothers and sisters, aunts, uncles, cousins, and parents on the job. All of us fall into one of these roles, depending on our position. We develop relationships with the people we work with, and those relationships need to be fed, watered, and nurtured, because we may spend as many years with our work mates as we do with some of our own family members.

Those of us in leadership positions have to be aware of the need to feed and water our working relationships with healthy servings of praise and appreciation for sincere, positive efforts. Firefighters respond well to a leader who doesn't demand respect or try to manage by making demands, but who rather earns respect through example and orchestrates the team to perform well as a unit. People do not want to be managed, but they do want to take ownership of their assignments and be allowed to discipline themselves to carry them out. Everyone should have that opportunity initially, and those who prove themselves unworthy of such a courtesy may have to be more closely observed down the road.

There should always be rewards for jobs well done, up and down the ladder. It's a two-way street, but it starts at the top, and all leaders should understand that their players need to know when they have done something good. We seem to be too quick to criticize and too slow to praise. The so-called rank-and-file members of an organization should also recognize when leaders have done something worth praising, and not be afraid to express that praise. It always seems easier for most of us to take shots at each other from both ends of the workplace spectrum. We seem to mostly accentuate the negative and point out what is wrong, rather than offer to be part of the solutions. It's that old team thing again.

Firefighters don't receive financial bonuses for saving lives and property, so it is important that they be appreciated for their efforts, if only in a small way, which usually works best. Most of us shy away from awards as we feel that we are only doing our job, but it is always a good morale boost and motivator to hear the boss say, "Job well done." It's not a bad thing for us to say the same back as well, when the boss deserves it. These words or similar words and gestures are needed to be heard and felt by everyone in the workforce, and it doesn't matter where we work or how much money we make.

In the fire service, we deal in situations that have to do with things that are a lot more important than wealth and other tangible things. We deal with things that are so important that a price could not possibly be put on them, and those we serve in these situations feel the same.

In the workplace, things of great importance that are priceless are respect and trust. People who earn these things have earned everything because trust and respect are everything in any relationship. They are the only things in the world that can be attained only by being earned. They cannot be stolen, inherited, tricked into, or bought, so leaders, treat the members of your team with sincere fairness because you can only go as far as they will go for you. Team members, do the same.

No one makes it alone, but we can blow it alone. As hard as it is to earn trust and respect, it is just as easy to lose them and harder to earn back. The key to blowing it is to fix it right away. It's okay for the boss or anyone else to say, "I'm sorry."

If we have earned the respect and trust of our teammates, no matter what our position is, we will reap dividends. Those dividends and bonuses should always have praise, and not in small doses. Praise should at least be balanced with criticism, or constructive feedback, but more praise can't hurt. Other forms of dividends can be whatever our imaginations can come up with that would fit a particular group. Thank you cards, flowers, cookies, lottery tickets, meals, or a day at the ballpark are just a few examples of little things that can make a big difference in our attitudes, morale, and how we approach our days at work. When the time comes for constructive feedback, discussions of certain issues and addressing challenges affecting the team, a foundation of trust and respect can already be laid for resolving those issues. Solutions can be emphasized in a positive environment that got that way through positive conditioning, and not because of the attitude of "my badge is bigger than yours."

The movie, *Remember the Titans,* is a story about a 1971 high school football team in Alexandria, Virginia, that was challenged to overcome many obstacles that had to do with attitude and approach. At one point during training camp, the head coach made the team go from two practices a day to three in an attempt to get the players to come together. After the third practice one night, Julius and Gary, two members of the defensive unit, get into a heated argument. Julius is a highly talented defensive end and Gary is an all-America linebacker and captain of the team.

Gary confronts Julius by telling him that he is tired of going through three practices a day because of the attitudes of people like Julius. Gary talks about how Julius and others like him are hurting the team. Julius comes back with his opinion of Gary's abilities as a captain and leader, that there is no team, and from now on he is going to look out only for himself. Gary's response to that is, "That's the worst attitude I've ever heard." Julius replies, "Attitude reflects leadership, Captain." From that moment on, things changed.

Attitude at work reflects leadership, period. It takes everyone to get it right, but it starts at the top. In the fire service, when a chief officer pulls up to the station in a filthy staff vehicle, one of three things will occur. One, and this is not likely to happen, the chief officer will wash the vehicle. Two, if the officer uses the size of his or her badge as a tool for getting things done, the crew will be asked, or told, to wash it. Three, if an environment of mutual trust and respect has been cultivated, the crew will drop what it's doing and wash that vehicle without a word being said by anyone. This is just an example of attitude reflecting leadership, and the same types of responses will occur whether it's washing cars or trying to save the same officer who became trapped in a burning building.

These theories apply to every working relationship in every kind of working situation, whether it's a small business, large corporation, or government entity. They apply in all aspects of our school systems, from the board to the principals to the teachers to the students. They are important in the classroom, performing arts stage, and athletic arena.

The creation of quality working relationships begins with quality leadership, but it doesn't end there because it takes the efforts of everyone involved. Remember, egos eat brains, attitude reflects leadership, and no one cares how much you know until they know how much you care.

# 10

# Reward Your Children, Reward Yourself

In any relationship we have that is important to us, we have to realize that they don't just happen by themselves. As we have discussed, they are built on foundations of earned trust and respect, and strengthened and maintained through proper nurturing, feeding, and watering.

Never is this more the case than with the relationships we have with our children. From the moment they are born, and even before, we are connected with them. They are dependent on us so much as infants and toddlers, and the interest we show or don't show them from the time they take their first breath registers and has a great deal to do with their development and happiness.

As our children grow and become more in touch with their social surroundings, their dependence on us as parents and guardians, but not as providers, will seem to diminish. So-called friends will take priority over family, and the time and attention we devoted to each other will likely now be directed, by our children, to others. They will have concerns over their popularity with their friends, and being accepted in these circles will have great importance.

This occurs in even the best of family environments, and we don't quite know when it's going to happen. It just seems to sneak up on us, and if we're lucky, it won't happen until high school. As difficult as this may be for us to deal with, as parents and guardians we have to decide just how much we should loosen the reins without letting go. It will be easier for some of us than it will be for others, and a lot will depend simply upon the foundation we have built. If it is one constructed out of earned mutual respect and trust, it will be a solid foundation. If we have built on that foundation a relationship of fair treatment, empowerment, ownership, and solid communication rather than one of control, ridicule and neglect, letting go enough will be easier. It is never easy, even if it is easier, but we need to allow ourselves to accept that our children need to explore these new regions that have sparked their interest. We can't be threatened by our children's growing and developing interests that are outside of the family. There are no guarantees, and we need to trust ourselves enough to feel we built relationships that are strong enough to keep us in our children's hearts and, most importantly, in their minds. If we have made ourselves available and approachable from day one, created a pleasant environment, and shown genuine interest in our children, chances are they will still long for the comfort of home, and our company. The other interests they have developed will be additions to the family, not replacements, and we can still be a big part of what our children want for themselves.

Based on solid foundations and strong relationships, if they find themselves in situations that create fear, discomfort, or otherwise raise questions about what is right, it is here that our children will either want to come home or they won't. Coming home can be literally or just in the heart and the mind, but if they choose to do so, all of the efforts we made will have been worthwhile.

Coming home in a figurative sense means our children will not allow themselves to purposely be put in dangerous situations, for they have already learned to stay away from them because of our influence, our respectfully talking with them, and their own learned ability to know what to do. Coming home is telling us about their new boyfriend or girlfriend because they want to share their discoveries and experiences with us. It's also their wanting to have friends over because they are as proud of us as we are of them. Besides, there isn't anywhere else they can get a better meal than the one they'll be sharing at home with their buddies.

We can't assume that our children will always do the right thing and will always be out of harm's way. Even though we have done everything we could possibly do to make sure they don't get hurt in many ways, there is still a chance that they will. However, we can bet the house that if we don't do what we need to do, if that foundation with our children is weak, they will most certainly take risks that carry heavy consequences. Our relationships with our children are tough and challenging responsibilities, even in the best of conditions. They are also potentially our most rewarding. In a sense, they are working relationships, demanding sound leadership qualifications, a fair structure of discipline, and a genuine sense of caring, which are all important in the development of a sound attitude.

The unique thing about the relationships we have with our children compared to anyone else is that in most cases we know them from the moment they are born. We have the opportunity to assist them in their development, also a requirement if that development is geared toward a quality human being. Unlike our relationships with our spouses, friends and other loved ones where we are introduced to them after their personalities have developed, and thus must adapt to them, we are a direct influence in the development of our children's personalities. The quality of the emotional and psychological environment that we provide for them is entirely up to us, and the happier we make our children, the happier we make ourselves. In essence, we are rewarding ourselves by being a major contributor in the development of a happy person. On the other hand, we are punishing our children if we do not utilize our opportunities in their development, and are thus punishing ourselves by having to face and live with the consequences.

Our children should be our best friends and we theirs, but it doesn't happen because we demand it. We get out of it what we put into it, on both sides, but we are the ones, as parents and guardians, who set the tone and attitude reflects leadership. We made the child in nine months, but it takes so much longer and a lot more work to construct the person. The building materials we use are up to us, so do we construct with straw or with concrete and re-enforced steel? Do we instill discipline because it is mutually understood that at times it is needed, or do we force it all the time because we think it's easier? When our children get into trouble, do we ask about what caused the problem that led to the trouble, as well as respond to the action (symptoms) that took place? A question or two asked out of concern for our best friend can help our friend make better decisions down the road. A pill will temporarily stop a runny nose, but healthy living will prevent the illness. Healthy living requires more of an effort, but always works better than a pill.

The ultimate test for us as parents is when it is time for our children to fly alone and be set free. It is then, with fingers crossed, that we find out if we balanced our time properly, had our priorities in order, and devoted ourselves to our children the way we should have, physically and emotionally. If they stay with us emotionally and have a good place for us in their minds and hearts, then we have succeeded.

# 11

# Wake-up Calls

The events following September 11, 2001, and people's behavior related to those events, were the result of a huge wake-up call that was heard not only in this country, but all over the world. For what seemed to be too brief a time, people's focus following the attacks was to go back to basics and simplicity, relationships and giving. It seemed as if the entire country, if not the world, was in a place of complete perspective, taken back by the horrific assaults that had occurred on our soil, and somehow forced into decency.

As unbelievable as it may sound, not everyone was touched by what happened, and as firefighters, we experienced some people who just plain slept through the whole thing. The phone was ringing right next to their ears, but they weren't about to wake up. In our own quaint and cozy little community, we experienced people ripping American flags off of our fire engines, heard people shouting support for those who attacked us, found expletives written in the streets denouncing our country, and were threatened with being fired for defending ourselves and our people from some of these actions. When we responded to the flurry of white powder spills and other malicious alarms that accompanied the following weeks, we were eventually accused of "knee jerking" and causing inconvenience to those who had gone back to sleep, or had never awakened in the first place. As time went by, we were made aware of similar experiences by other fire departments and other people in general.

A few short months after the attacks and into a war that we continue to fight and incur losses, it seems as if a lot of people have forgotten the promises they made on September 11. Many of us who are far away from Ground Zero and the Pentagon, or not affected by a great loss from them have gone back to September 10, or just stayed there. The flags we waved and displayed have become tattered, faded, and worn out, just as the promises we made, and many have gone back to sleep until the next wake-up call. Hollywood pulled its films about terrorism and other violence in September, but they're all back now, and then some. Major league baseball's attention is on another strike, who should throw at whom, and steroid use. General ethics appear to be nonexistent. Martha Stewart, corporate executives, and representatives of the cloth are being investigated for any number of crimes, and drivers on the highways all hate each other. Are these examples of where we wanted to be when we got back to normal?

The most unfortunate thing about all this, next to the tremendous loss of life and the suffering of loved ones left behind, are the opportunities that a lot of people failed to recognize and take advantage of. Wake-up calls are meant to wake us up, and if we go right back to sleep after receiving one, we are going to miss that very important meeting with the chance to better ourselves. Most of us don't have to do a complete makeover, but re-evaluating some of our priorities could sure help. A lot of us made a lot of promises on September 11 and now it's up to us to live up to them.

Maybe someday we'll be able to produce and maintain some reasonable perspective in our lives without the loss of a friend, loved one, or 343 of our brothers and sisters.

# 12

# Avoid Unhappy People and Conditional Love

One of the best wake-up calls any of us can receive is the one telling us to get up and walk away from anyone who brings us down. It's a call we usually have to make to ourselves, even though the phone next to us may have been ringing for quite some time.

These people are simply unhappy, yet they complicate our lives to no end and make us unhappy as well, as if it is their goal. They are definitely in need of a wake-up call, but they have put cotton in their ears before applying the ear muffs, so there's no way they can hear the phone ring. They spin a contagious web of misery that we can easily get caught in and eventually become ill from. They long for things and people that won't do any good and attempt to fill voids with superficial things that are unfulfilling. It seems as if everything they do is because of someone else's efforts or at someone else's expense. They are needy, do not like themselves, are harmful to themselves and others, but at the same time are extremely selfish. Everything is about them, and they have no concern for what their action and behavior do to others. They are easily bored when not being entertained and easily boring to those with a clue. Though in need, they do not want help, guidance, or a way out of their misery, and justify that misery by blaming others for being stuck where they are. Their relationships are based on need, control, and lies and not on mutual respect and trust.

We, on the other hand, have a tendency to respond to all of this by blaming ourselves for their problems in spite of our good intentions. We feel that we have to try and fix or rescue these types of people, and work very hard at it. They don't want to be rescued, but they won't tell us this until they have exhausted us and tossed us aside in favor of new performers. Feeling as failures, we subconsciously look for other distressed souls to save and work harder to try and fix what cannot be fixed. We keep trying to repair things or just keep them from breaking any more with continued exhausting performances of giving in attempts to win affection and acceptance, but we just become more trapped in the web.

Trying to be Superman, or Superwoman, we end up developing and repeating familiar, vicious, and seemingly endless patterns, but instead of having a red "S" stamped to our chest, we are just stamped "Unhappy Person." This label has more clout than the Good Housekeeping Seal of Approval, because approval is the best we could hope for from these people, and now we are one of them. If they like what we are doing, our behavior has their approval, for the moment, and that's it. We could behave the same way tomorrow and it's disapproved of. The wrong word, expression, or intent perceived by these people put us right back in the doghouse, only there's no dog in there for us to hug. We are left worn out, frustrated, angry, and confused looking for a way to fix it, thus the cycle and pattern starts again.

This is our wake-up call, but we need to hear it, get up, relieve ourselves, and run, not walk, but *run* away from the clutches of this web. It may take years to hear the phone ring, but once we hear it, and it's never too late, it's time to

54

wake up. The web is only as strong as we allow it to be, for all it takes is the first step. We can't make them happy, and we didn't make them unhappy.

It takes some of us a long time to realize that we are attracted to unhappy people and that we are unhappy ourselves. What counts is that we are able to eventually realize it and then do something about it. It may involve being alone for a while, and it may very well hurt, but the day will come when we are okay with it. When we feel happy about ourselves, by ourselves, that is when we'll feel the big red S on our chest. The so-called seal of approval will fade away, and we will attract, and be attracted to, happier people. We will be okay with or without people, and being alone will not mean feeling lonely.

Our lives are made up of choices, and whether we control ourselves or are controlled by others, they're our choices. If we're nice or we're not nice, we're happy or not happy, they're our choices. Others may influence us, but the decisions to be who we are belong to us. Some of us may feel trapped and honestly believe there is no way out of a particular situation, but only we can determine when it is worth it to break out of the web. If it is that bad, then it's worth it, so make the move. All it takes are some guts and the first step, so hear the phone, wake up, take the call, and listen to the voice.

# 13

# Be Easy to Help

There are two kinds of people in the world, those in counseling and those who should be.

Upon returning from New York City in the aftermath of September 11, 2001, each member of the Sacramento Urban Search and Rescue Team (USAR) was awarded a credit toward $10,000 of counseling, in addition to the Critical Incident Stress Debriefings (CISD) that were already being provided. My brother Andoni is on that team along with several other members who are good friends and colleagues, namely Larry, Jeff, and Darrin. I am so proud of all of them, and happy and thankful that they returned safely. I am also proud and honored for the privilege of being able to work with them from time to time.

For firefighters, counseling is a valuable tool to help us maintain our mental stability that is challenged from time to time as a result of the experiences we live through on the job. It is a part of our normal existence and is not looked upon as something that is associated solely with mental illness or a sign of weakness for those who seek it. In fact, it is a vital source for healthy living and a good way to prevent mental illness. Lucy Van Pelt of the comic strip Peanuts once said in reference to counseling, "The fact that you admit there might be a problem indicates that you are not too far gone."

All people are exposed to things every day that can cause depression, concern, fear, anger, and loss of perspective, control, and a sense of reality. This doesn't necessarily mean that everyone should seek professional counseling (that's up to the individual), but everyone does need help and support of some sort. If we are fortunate enough to have people in our lives who genuinely care about us, they will want to constructively help us feel better about the things that get us down and challenge us (and we will for them). The key is to let them help, to accept and trust what they are trying to do for us, and to at least try some of the suggested methods that may be offered and work best for us. Others may be able to see what we can't, and a lot of times a suggestion from someone else toward a possible solution will put us on the path that will help us find that solution ourselves.

Solutions should not be looked upon as cures for our problems, but as ways to help us get through, accept and deal with a problem. Only we can cure ourselves of anything, and that comes from inside of us, but there is nothing wrong with getting some help along the way. A captain or chief officer can always use another set of eyes on the fire ground, which can help address the problems being faced. A good counselor (professional or otherwise) will not try to cure anyone, but will offer coping mechanisms that can be used as tools for getting direction on how to work with a problem and get through it.

A lot of things that bother us are things that we have absolutely no control over, and accepting this is a huge step towards feeling better. We cannot change what we cannot control, so the best we can hope for is that it will change on its own. What we can do in the meantime is change how we deal with it by perhaps not exposing ourselves to it or by approaching it with a different attitude. Sometimes all it takes is something as simple as turning off or changing the channel on the radio or television, or otherwise controlling what we do have control over. Another approach may be realizing that people who cause us mental strain and anguish usually have much bigger problems than the ones we are letting them create for us. This might be just the solution we are looking for. Finally, we may be the source of our own problems, and when we decide to do something about us, we have begun arriving at solutions. Charlie Brown would be proud.

Sadly, a lot of us see accepting counseling, or sound advice from friends and loved ones as a threat or sign of weakness in ourselves. For this reason we do not seek it, accept it, or otherwise allow ourselves opportunities to resolve issues and feel better, and we become or remain unhappy. We waste a lot of time being stuck simply because we think we can solve the problem ourselves, or we deny the whole thing and try to convince ourselves and others that there is no problem.

In order to solve a problem we may have, we have to accept it and then do something about it. However, acceptance only comes after we deny there is a problem, isolate ourselves with it ("it's all about me"), become angry and depressed because nobody understands, bargain with it ("oh, just one little drink won't hurt"), and finally accept it. How quickly we solve or deal with our problems may very well depend on our willingness to embrace counseling, whether from a friend, professional, a loved one or all three. The first step is always the hardest, but it has to come from inside of us in order to achieve a successful solution. It cannot be forced as the result of a plea, threat, or ultimatum from someone else. As hard as that first step may be, it is the biggest and most significant, and each step following makes the journey easier and shorter.

Most of the time there is no cure and the journey never ends, but that doesn't necessarily mean failure. Remember, solutions are not cures. Finding a way to manage a problem and live with it constructively is certainly a challenge, but no less rewarding than solving it, should that ever happen. The rewards are in the efforts we make, and though it may be a never-ending journey, it will become smoother with each passing day.

A large key to making the journey smoother is to let people help us, to be easy to help. Without support systems, and there are many out there for many different situations (ask about them), we are cheating ourselves of opportunities that can change our lives and put us in a better place.

Don't be afraid to ask for help, for you just might get it.

# 14

# When Dreams Don't Come True

All of us have had childhood dreams of accomplishing great things, such as gracing the silver screen as a famous actor or actress or playing for the Yankees or Mets and following the footsteps of Mickey Mantle, Babe Ruth, Joe DiMaggio, and George Theodore. We grow up to be a scientist who discovers the cure for a deadly disease, or a teacher in Denver who earns the love and respect from the hearts of thousands of students. Each night when we fall asleep we become the director of a symphony, the quarterback of our favorite football team or the commander of the United States Air Force Thunderbirds. Some of us have been fortunate enough to see our childhood dreams come true, but for most of us, they have remained dreams.

Our dreams are as special to us as a close friend or a true love, but at some point we have to realize that they are not going to come true. A lot of us go through a grieving process that lasts a lifetime, and we never allow ourselves to get over it. We mourn the death of our dream longer than we would ever grieve over the loss of someone or something real that meant more. Grief trapped in the heart turns to anger, which prevents us from moving on to new opportunities. Anger doesn't change anything; it just stifles us.

In dealing with a loss we normally go through periods of adjustment that involve mourning, and we eventually return to a sense of "normalcy." Though we have lost something dear to us, we should, after a reasonable amount of time, reach a point where we need to resume our lives in the ways they are supposed to be lived. We need to accept what has happened and allow ourselves to pursue new dreams, embrace new opportunities, and harvest new rewards. The fact that our dream did not materialize could very well have been something we had no control over. We may choose to see it as an injustice toward us, something that wasn't meant to be, or with a more positive approach, something that will direct us toward a new dream.

We may not have been good enough to play pro ball, but if we gave up after only that one dream, we would have never become a firefighter and volunteer high school baseball coach for our alma mater, things that may turn out to be more worthwhile. We wouldn't have helped shape the lives of the kids we coached and watch them go on to become pro ballplayers themselves, or teachers, business people, and firefighters as well. They wouldn't be coming by the house years after graduation to clean our yard "just because," and they wouldn't ask to use our study to prepare for their broker's exam. Had we spent the rest of our lives fretting over the one sweetheart who dumped us, we wouldn't have attracted that wonderful person who fell so madly in love with us, and vice versa.

With each ending there are new beginnings, and realizing they are out there is like being born again.

# 15

# Empower Others, Empower Yourself

From time to time, each of us finds ourselves in leadership roles where we are in charge of reaching goals through the help of others. Most of us are in those positions every day in some form, as the general manager of a grocery store, the foreman of a factory crew, the coach of a baseball team, captain of a fire engine company, or the leader in a household or other situations of our personal lives. Whether we are baby-sitting our little sister or running a corporation, two things remain constant. First, people want leadership, and second, they don't want to be managed.

Our time needs to be managed, but our people need to be empowered and given ownership of their duties, projects, assignments, and overall team goals. Our little sister doesn't want to be told what to do every minute, and our employees and coworkers don't want us looking over their shoulders for eight hours to make sure they are following orders. What our little sister wants is to be directed to go in her room and play with her toys, watch a video in the living room, make cookies with us in the kitchen or do anything reasonable that will occupy her time productively and provide her with enjoyment. What our employees, workmates, and crewmembers want are to be assigned provocative, worthwhile projects and duties, with some general guidance from us toward the team's overall objective. They then want to be left alone to pursue that objective, with our role being that of an orchestrator and a helper when needed.

Micromanagement, whether in baby-sitting or directing a group of teammates or coworkers, is a morale buster at any level. A big part of our job as leaders is to let our people know that the projects and duties they have are to be managed by them and their colleagues. We are there to help plan and outline the objectives and goals of the project, to assist when needed and to provide support if and when there is a needed change in the original plan. Changes might include a needed deadline extension, obtaining additional resources, or finding answers to questions that may surface or were not considered prior.

There may be times when a project that needs to be done is met with resistance because it may not present the types of challenges that will motivate most people, or is just no fun. These types of projects should have enough participation from the leaders to the point where the other team members believe that the leaders would not ask someone to do what they would not do themselves. It doesn't hurt for the fire captain to clean the bathroom now and then, for it's this type of action and attitude that builds a foundation of mutual respect and makes the team feel that the leaders really care. The team will stand up for the leader, and the leader will do the same for the team.

Doing the little things helps people believe that the big things will get done as well. When we're finished making the cookies with our little sister, we can help with the cleanup and not just tell her to do it herself. Little things such as praising a job well done or just saying "thank you" for the effort are other ways to empower those we lead, whether on the job or at home. In the fire service, unexpected rewards such as the captain cooking dinner for the crew, taking them to a ballgame, springing for mochas or buying everyone a lottery ticket go a long way. This helps motivate and bind the team together for anything, whether it's the project at hand, routine chores, or a major incident.

When we empower others, we are challenging them in a most positive way to become the owners of a project, assignment or goal. We provide opportunities for success and responsibilities for one's own actions, as opposed to threatening ultimatums if orders and assignments are not carried out to certain specifications, or by constantly supervising and scrutinizing every move. The use of discipline and constant intervention should be last resorts of leadership practices and not normal methods of operation for those in leadership positions. The power that good leaders provide can only come back in the form of power as well. Mutual trust and respect surface and grow in this environment as has been proven in many situations when leaders take this approach with a responsible team. It is telling the team members that their leader will protect and support them in any situation. This helps develop a team that is dedicated to proving itself worthy as well as a team that will do practically anything to protect and support its leaders. Leaders who show respect for their team provide the most power and receive the most in return. When a teammate asks a question, the leader answers in a way that keeps the flow of power moving back and forth. The leader does not foreclose on the ownership by making the teammate feel he or she should have known the answer all along, and since the leader, or manager in this case, knew the answer, that is why the teammate is the subordinate.

Here is an example of a hypothetical situation in the fire service, presented two ways, which can either empower a team, or inhibit it, depending on the approach of the leader.

The fire department has just been given approval to purchase a new fire engine. The chief has announced the news at a staff meeting and has asked for a member of the staff to head the project. A captain offers to take the job, and after the staff meeting the chief and the captain have a private meeting later in the day to discuss the project.

This is the first approach to the situation, where leadership does not offer empowerment and ownership.

Chief: "Captain, here's what I would like you to do with this project. I want you to set up meetings with representatives of the manufacturers on this list that I have made up. You and I will travel to each factory and see the operation, as well as find out what each company has to offer. I want the best job for the least amount of money, and I want to see who will offer the most in the way of 'free extras.' I will talk to them about that once we meet in person. I have made a set of specifications that I want on this engine, and I do not want to deviate from them. With my years of experience I know what should be on a fire engine."

Captain: "Chief, should we get some input from our engineers and other firefighters as to what they feel our needs are as far as a new engine?"

Chief: "That is not necessary since I have already decided that. Here are the dates that I want us to travel next month, which should give you enough time to set up the meetings."

Captain: "I've noticed that there are some good quality manufacturers that are not on this list you have given me."

Chief: "Just make the necessary arrangements with what I have given you. That is all."

Captain: "Yes, sir."

Here is the second approach, where empowerment

and ownership are offered, thus providing a two-way street.

Chief: "Captain, thank you for taking on this project. It's great that we are finally going to have the new engine that we've needed for so long, and I'm glad someone like yourself is in charge of this project."

Captain: "Thank you, Chief."

Chief: "I want you to form a staff to work with you on putting this together. The only input I have at this time is for you and your team to consider that this engine will be with us for the next thirty years. Plan accordingly as far as cabinet and storage space and the type of equipment we'll need to carry. City Hall is requiring us to get at least three bids, but I'm leaving it up to you if you need to involve more vendors."

Captain: "Do you want to be included in the committee?"

Chief: "Not necessarily, but if you could please provide me with periodic updates, that would probably be sufficient. Also, if you have questions or need any guidance, don't hesitate to contact me."

Captain: "That sounds good, but your input is valuable and you are invited to attend whatever meetings you are able to make."

Chief: "Thank you, I'll keep that in mind."

Captain: "Do you have any specific requests at this time?"

Chief: "No. This is your project and your department's engine. I trust you will make sound decisions based on your team's input and whatever assistance I can provide."

Captain: "Thank you for your faith and trust."

Chief: "Good luck, Captain."

Which scenario would you rather be a part of, either as

the chief or the captain, and which scenario provides power and ownership to both parties?

Realizing our goals doesn't mean a thing if they come at the expense of the people we live with, work with, and care about. They shouldn't come at anyone's expense for that matter. Poor treatment of the people we are around and come in contact with will result in consequences for us somewhere down the line. That's just the way it works and the way it's supposed to work. Who we really are will eventually surface, and people will either see the goodness or see through the facade. If we want to be effective leaders or just good people, we have to do it right and we have to do it with sincerity. What goes around comes around, and our abilities as a corporate head, parent, fire chief, ball player, or super genius will only go so far in getting people to respond to us. Those abilities and positions by themselves will not do the job, but who we are, not what we do or what we're good at will be the determining factor as to how far people will go for us in any situation. The use of control and influence may get results, but it comes at a price and with diminishing returns the longer this type of system is in place.

The quality of our personalities and the strength of our foundations are what give life to us and to those around us, in any situation. They are the difference in our abilities as leaders (we are all leaders at some time during the day) and in the quality of our relationships. Our personalities can always be polished, and depending on how dull the finish was to start with, the time it takes to obtain or keep the shine will vary. Our foundations can also be restructured, and repairing the cracks, removing the rubble, and filling the voids will take time as well. However, it's never too late for any of us to take the time to make ourselves stronger and more personable, because whether we realize it or not,

not being decent, fair, and nice is just as bad for us as it is for those around us. This may sound as if it came from one of "Barney" the dinosaur's lectures, but it's true. Ever notice how people who routinely treat people poorly have an especially hard time when they are treated the same way, even though it may very well be justified?

There are no guarantees that providing ownership and empowering those around us will always work in the different leadership roles we find ourselves in every day. Whether we're in this role 24/7 or just a few minutes a day, this approach can create opportunities and challenge people to succeed and respond with a positive approach from both sides. Where it goes from there is up to the individual or the team being led, and whether our role continues as a leader or becomes that of a manager is up to them. One thing is guaranteed, and that is no one cares how much you know until they know how much you care.

# 16

# Choose Your Heroes Carefully

Whether we realize it or not, the people we look up to are those we perceive to have great character. What we sometimes do though, especially in our society, is to mistake too many things for character and goodness. We look at a person's ability, talent, social or celebrity status, what a person does for a living, among many other things, as good and rich with character. What a lot of us fail to realize is that character and goodness are separate qualities, or at least should be goals for all of us. They are, or are not a large part of who and what we are, but are not extensions of the tangible segments of our identity.

The fact that a person is a tremendous athlete, gifted artist, glamorous performer, influential businessperson, or even a firefighter who risks his or her life daily for others does not automatically qualify that person as full of goodness and rich in character. A deeply religious person, someone who is nice and/or loves his or her family does not automatically qualify as good. If a person happens to be good in addition to being in a fortunate, privileged, or respected position, then that person is certainly worthy of our admiration or so-called hero status, provided it is earned.

Most of us choose our heroes too easily, and the qualifications we require of them are not stringent enough. A true hero helps to shape people's lives in a positive way over time. If we are in need of heroes, as many of us seem to be, it's best to look in the right place for the right type of person. Good places to start looking are in the mirror and in our own hearts. If we like what we find, there may not be a need to look any further. Shaping our own lives in a positive way often takes a heroic effort, and if we are able to accomplish this, especially against long odds or a rough start, then we have established high standards and should not settle for less.

The key is to choose a hero who is worthy of who we want to be, and not aim too low. If we think we want to be a gangster, then we'll choose someone who fits that mold. If this is as high as we are aiming, then it's a good opportunity to look in the mirror and into the heart. Most certainly, these "heroes" will at best disappoint us and, and at worst bury us. By looking to our self first and realizing there is a better way, we have just become our own hero.

We place huge responsibilities on the heroes we choose, and if they don't come through for us as we might hope, we are extremely disappointed, and sometimes broken-hearted. There may be times when even heroes need heroes, and with all the demands made upon him, even Superman needs someone to turn to from time to time. Usually it's his parents.

In the movie, *A Bronx Tale*, Sonny, the neighborhood thug, wins the admiration of a ten-year-old boy named Calogero, or C as Sonny prefers to call him. After C witnesses Sonny kill a man in the street during an argument, and then refuses to "snitch" to the police during questioning, Sonny takes the boy under his wing. Against the wishes of the young man's father, a bus driver who despises Sonny, the gangster and the boy spend a lot of time together and C learns about, and is impressed by, the charmed life

70

Sonny seems to live as an organized crime boss. During this time, C also looks down on his father for the job and lifestyle he has chosen, referring to him as a "sucker," in Sonny's words. Sonny then becomes C's hero, even though he is a bad man who does bad things.

Early in their relationship, Sonny talks to C after Pittsburgh's Bill Mazeroski hit the dramatic home run to defeat the New York Yankees in game seven of the 1960 World Series. C is upset because his baseball idol, Mickey Mantle, cried after losing the series. Sonny asked C if he thought Mantle cared as much about people such as C, as C did about the Yankee centerfielder.

"How much money does your father make?" Sonny asked the boy.

"I don't know," replied C.

"Mickey Mantle makes $100,000 a year. Do you think he would care about you if your father couldn't pay the rent? He doesn't care. Nobody cares!"

By the time they were finished talking, C was convinced that ball players don't care about regular folks to the point where the kid wanted to throw away all his baseball cards.

As several years go by, Sonny looks after C and actually saves his life at one point. However, had it not been for Sonny's influence, C would not have needed to be saved.

In the end, Sonny eventually pays dearly for his ways, and fortunately for C, he lives to make wiser decisions. He finally sees his father, a good and decent man, as the real hero, and he no longer cares about what he does for a living.

As far as our heroes caring about us, it would be nice if they did, for a true hero does. If we choose them carefully, respecting ourselves in the process, there is a fair chance they will care.

Should we be disappointed if our favorite sports personalities, entertainers, or whoever don't really care about us? No. Although it would be nice if they showed greater appreciation for what we do for them (the same way salespeople should do for their customers), there is no reason for them to care about us with the same amount of passion and energy that we seem to want to spend on them. What we need to do is tone it down a bit, empower ourselves and take control of our emotions and the situation, whatever it happens to be. If enough of us respond appropriately after the next strike by the oppressed overprivileged, things might end up more balanced and equitable. We can still have fun reading the box scores, preparing for next Sunday's N.F.L. match-ups, standing in line for that movie we've been waiting for, phoning the sports talk radio show, and going to concerts and plays. Enjoy the game, the show, or the performance, but when it's over, win or lose, it's over. Look forward to the next one, but in the meantime, go home to the life you hopefully have. The ballplayers are not going to spend the week worrying about the guy in Section 105, Row 1, who wears his favorite players' jersey and just got laid off from his job. Those of us who seriously put so much emphasis into what others are doing might want to focus a little more on our own lives and try and connect with the greatest hero of them all, our self.

Sure, Fan Appreciation Day should be observed every day, but until that happens, let's take back some power and hang onto it. Start by not asking for autographs, especially the adults, and quit kissing up to them in every other way imaginable to the point where they honestly believe the press conferences they call are important and people want to hear them. What if nobody showed up and people didn't want to read or hear about them? Of course, not all of our arena heroes are like this, and some of them do good things for more reasons than just a tax break and a headline.

The most important things to consider in our lesson in hero-worship awareness are character and goodness in the people we turn to. When we really need a true hero, we won't be thinking about home runs, movie scenes, touch-downs, three pointers, songs, golf shots, or the latest trends. We'll be longing for where and with whom we feel the safest and strongest, and if we are strong as well, we will be part of the equation.

# 17

# Never Give Up

This book has touched on several different types of situations that we all experience and are exposed to from time to time. It has dealt with some of the challenges we face in our daily lives and has offered some suggestions on how to possibly approach them. Most of what the book discusses are the choices we make in our lives and how they might affect us. We have compared life's choices to playing in a baseball game or traveling on a journey, offered ways of gaining inspiration from children and the elderly, and suggested methods for maintaining and strengthening relationships. In the journey we are traveling, we look in figurative terms to the different parts of our body and how they can best guide us to where we would like to be. We invoke healthy methods of selfishness not as apathetic approaches with regards to others, but as formulas for helping us constructively care for others.

No matter where we live and work or where our daily journeys take us, we find ourselves in the roles as leaders at some time during each day. We talk about the importance of incorporating teamwork and empowerment into our interactions with family, friends, coworkers, and strangers, and how this makes things better for everyone we come in contact with, including ourselves.

In addition to life's comparisons to baseball and travel,

we look at different situations from the perspective of a firefighting crew through first-hand experiences. References to September 11, 2001, are used as reminders to all of us of our potential for greatness as individuals and as a nation. You, as the reader, may have your own set of examples that you are familiar and comfortable with in your own comparisons to life's games and travels. Whatever they happen to be, they do offer perspective for anyone with an open mind.

We discuss how, although we may be a part of one person's happiness, we are not the cause of another's unhappiness and are not responsible for it. Those of us who have the courage to seek counseling from either a professional or a friend have learned that not finding a cure for our problems is not failure, and that success is finding a new approach to them. And just because our dreams don't always come true does not mean that the door is closed to pursue others. Finally we suggest that we set high standards when looking for a hero, then check the mirror or the nearest children's hospital before looking any further.

Before closing, I would like to discuss one more important thing that compares to, yes, baseball, life's journeys, and the fire department. "Never give up."

These three words are the foundation of the fire service, in my opinion. No matter how routine or catastrophic an incident happens to be, it is our duty to push forward and find a way to get the job done. Just as in our everyday lives, sometimes things can be so intense that we need help, but we ask for it, and get it. We may also have to make adjustments in our approach to better handle the incident, but we will make them and never give up.

In New York City, since September 11, the F.D.N.Y, in addition to the 343 lives that were lost on that day, has had to hire close to one thousand new firefighters to fill the spots vacated by those who were injured and were unable to return, and those who retired for a variety of reasons. Those who left did so because they could not do the job anymore, not because they would not do it. They did not give up. The department knows this and will not allow these new firefighters to become any less than the people who were there before them.

In life's journey we must never give up even though the road will many times be rough and challenging. There will most likely be detours in our journey, which may come in the form of any or all of tragedy, loss, not realizing a dream, illness, realizing a dream, good fortune, and fate. We never know what tomorrow will bring, so as long as we have tomorrows and a good approach, we will always have something to look forward to.

My friends Frank and Sannie had a son, Frank Jr., who in 1988 was touted as a "can't miss" baseball-pitching prospect during his senior year of high school. His fastball was clocked consistently above ninety miles per hour with the type of movement that was rare coming from a player at this level. With a bright future on the horizon, Frank planned to enroll in the fall at the University of California at Berkeley.

Frankie, as he was known, was so much more than an exceptional ballplayer. He had a great personality, a tremendous sense of humor, and was an inspiration to everyone around him. He was the epitome of the subject matter in chapter 3, as were Danny, my nephew, and Danny's grandfather, my dad.

One day at school, between classes, Frankie approached one of the teachers on the school grounds. Showing his talent for comedy, he said to the teacher, "I'm going to steal the English building."

"What?" asked the teacher.

"I'm . . . going . . . to steal . . . the English building!"

"This I would like to see."

The instant the teacher finished his challenge, Frankie sprinted toward the building, slid into the wall, jumped up, turned to face the teacher, and imitating a baseball umpire, extended and crossed his arms in front of him palms down, then brought his arms out to each side parallel to the ground, yelling "*Safe!*"

Just after the preseason part of the baseball season in the spring of 1988, in which Frankie sported an earned run average of below one, he went to the dentist for some minor oral surgery. When the cuts in his mouth did not heal in a timely manner, the dentist advised his parents to take him for some blood tests. At this time, it was discovered that Frankie had leukemia. Now he was involved in a different game.

Frankie approached his illness with the same passion and intensity he exhibited on the mound when facing an opposing batter. His attitude in baseball was "never give up, never give an inch," and this same attitude helped him battle the disease for the next two-and-one-half years. However, his baseball career wasn't over yet.

During the same season in which he was diagnosed, Frankie's team made it to the postseason playoffs. His younger brother Gabe (currently a Triple-A professional pitcher with the Texas Rangers) was brought up from the junior varsity and put in the rotation in Frankie's spot. The contributions made by Gabe were significant in the team's success, which was fueled by Frankie's inspiration.

He was with the team for the playoffs a week after the completion of a series of spinal taps and chemotherapy treatments. Dressed in street clothes, Frankie rooted his team to a first-round victory while on a roller coaster of emotions. The professional scouts attending the game received a huge dose of his comedy when he told them, "Those radar guns you kept pointing at me gave me cancer." By the end of the game, Frankie, alone in the dugout with just his coach, began to cry and said, "Coach, I want to play."

In the second round of the playoffs, Frankie's team fell behind early in a game that meant the loser had its season end. He kept looking at the coach the same way he did after the first game, again in his street clothes. In the fifth inning with no outs and the bases loaded, still behind and on defense, a coaching decision was made that had nothing to do with baseball. The coach took off his own uniform jersey, handed it to Frank, and nodded his head.

When Frankie entered the field and took the mound, the cheers and standing ovation of not only his own rooters, but his opponent's as well had nothing to do with baseball. In spite of all the treatments, no practice, significant loss of velocity in his pitches, and the odds, Frankie retired the side giving up no runs and striking out a batter. It was his last game.

During his subsequent battles against this dreaded disease, Frankie never got caught up in feeling sorry for himself. There were many serious and unfair challenges, but he always focused on his blessings and the great life he had. The only thing that visibly bothered him was seeing the children he was in touch with in the hospital fighting the same battles. In similar fashion, my father responded by saying, with tears in his eyes, after learning that his grandson also had cancer, "I have no problem with what's happened to me, but here there is no justice." From that point, they both fought it together, without a hint of self-pity.

Frankie lost his battle with leukemia on October 7, 1990. His family continues the fight that he fought so hard

and with so much dignity. Each year a baseball tournament, hosted and sponsored by Frankie's family and the
community, is held on Memorial Day weekend to bring
kids together to play ball. The tournament is played on the
home field of Frankie's high school, which now carries his
name. At the entrance to the ballpark is a bronze statue of
Frankie, where before the first home game of the high
school season the team gathers around the statue to say a
prayer. And before each game of the memorial tournament,
a child who has battled or is currently battling a
life-threatening disease throws out the first pitch. My
nephew Danny participates in this ceremony, which every
year is inspired by everything Frankie's life was all about.

This book and my life have been inspired by people
such as Frankie, Danny, my dad, Jones, my family, friends,
and my wonderful wife Amber. They have inspired and
challenged me to focus on my blessings and the important
things I have instead of dwelling on the unimportant
things I don't have. I feel very fortunate to have this kind of
guidance in the choices I make, but I took the first step and
continue to work hard at it. Those are the only ways to do it
right in my opinion. Even the people I don't know, but
come in contact with every day provide me with great challenges to try and be as good a person as possible. Some
days are better than others, and for me the whole thing is a
ballgame. They still throw at my head, but the tendency to
want to charge the mound does not come with the same frequency it once did.

The movie *Mr. Mom* is a story about a family where the
husband and wife switch roles after he gets laid off from
his job as an automobile executive. The wife gets a job as an
advertising executive, and the husband becomes a
stay-at-home dad. After they have been in their new roles
for a while, the wife has become obsessed with her work

and starts losing touch with the things that once meant so much to her, mostly her family. For Halloween, the family had made plans to all go trick-or-treating together, including the parents. At the last minute, the mom is told by her boss that she needs to fly across the country to assist in the making of a commercial. The entire family is extremely disappointed, thinking again that Mom doesn't care. As the mom is getting ready to board the limo to go to the airport, the dad says, "You gave me some really good advice once. You said, 'It's really easy to forget what's important, so don't.' "

I hope you have the good fortune you truly deserve, but if your journey has wandered off course or you're in a slump, grab the wheel and get back in the right direction, keep swinging away, and never give up, because we are the navigators of our souls.

# About the Author

## Written by Andoni Kastros, Mitch's Brother

Mitch Kastros is a hero to his family, but not the type to re-cite his resume or adorn his walls with self-gratifying cer-tificates and recognition. So I, his little brother, wrote this for him.

He is the most loving and down-to-earth, sometimes subterranean, person you would ever love to meet. Mitch is a fire captain with the Carmel Fire Department, and has been in the fire service for over twenty-nine years. Both of his brothers are firefighters as well, inspired by our dad and each other.

Although he is in his fifties, the oldest son of six chil-dren in a "Big Fat Greek" family, Mitch is still a kid. He loves Warner Brothers cartoons (he has close to every one ever made; Bugs Bunny, Road Runner, Sylvester, Foghorn Leghorn and the rest), great food, family and all the good things to do with baseball. Most, if not all, of his rare lei-sure time is involved with one of these simple pleasures while hanging out at home with his wife, Amber, and their animals.

His so-called hobbies involve making other people feel good, such as towing his barbecue trailer to events to feed hundreds of lucky hungry folks. He was a volunteer assis-tant baseball coach for nine years for his alma mater, Carmel High. He doesn't know how many league championships they won, but there were several, including one sectional crown and a Number One state ranking. The best part of Mitch's coaching career is seeing how many of his former players keep in touch by calling, dropping by the house or the fire station to say "hi," and usually ending up staying for dinner.

He has a special fondness for children, and with his family and job, contributes in many ways to children's causes, especially in the fight against cancer and leukemia. The fire department is a frequent contributor to fundraisers, which benefit area schools and other children's causes.

Mitch is my hero and, through being blessed, was with me and participated on two out of the three "career calls" I have been on. The third was September 11, 2001 in New York, and though he was not physically with me, he was there just the same. His daily phone calls kept me focused and inspired during a time when I otherwise would have felt alone and helpless.

Chances are, if you ever said "hi" to Mitch on the street, he would thank you for spending the time and insist you and twenty of your closest friends come over for a small steak, baby back rib, and chicken barbecue, complete with side-dishes, and cheeseburgers for dessert. That's just Mitch, painfully kind with the biggest heart of anyone on earth. His child-like love of life and almost naïve kindness towards people make him truly one-of-a-kind.